FINANCIAL *freedom in* 8 *minutes* a DAY

HOW TO ATTRACT AND MANAGE ALL THE MONEY YOU'LL EVER NEED

Ron Hulnick, Ph.D.
& Mary Hulnick, Ph.D.

Rodale Press
Emmaus, Pennsylvania

NOTICE

The information contained in this book is based upon the authors' personal experience as well as their professional experience in working with clients. It is intended for use as an approach to deal with the many day-to-day decisions we all make regarding the wise use of our money. It is not in any way intended for investment purposes, nor are the authors or publisher in any way responsible for the results the individual obtains through its use.

Editor: David Parke Epstein
Cover and Book Designer: Jane Colby Knutila
Illustrator: Cathie Bleck
Technical Illustrator: Academy Artworks, Inc.
Cover Photographers: John P. Hamel (sky); Mitch Mandel (clock)

Library of Congress Cataloging-in-Publication Data

Hulnick, Ron.
   Financial freedom in 8 minutes a day : how to attract and manage all the money you'll ever need / Ron Hulnick and Mary Hulnick.
     p.   cm.
   Includes index.
   ISBN 0–87596–189–4 hardcover
1. Finance, Personal. I. Hulnick, Mary. II. Title. III. Title: Financial freedom in eight minutes day.
HG179.H847 1994
332.024—dc20   93–34997
                                          CIP

Distributed in the book trade by St. Martin's Press

2 4 6 8 10 9 7 5 3 1 hardcover

To all those who understand that
the real purpose of money is to
assist us in fulfilling our dreams

CONTENTS

PART III   THINK WEALTHY, FEEL WEALTHY,
BE WEALTHY

ACKNOWLEDGMENTS

If you seek a humbling experience, write a book. You will soon find out it is not something you can do all by yourself. And so we'd like to thank those who played an important role in helping us bring this book to press.

First and foremost, we are grateful to our parents, Charles and Ida Hulnick and Henry and Helen Holverson, who taught us the habits of wise stewardship of money. Their early guidance no doubt contributed to the commonsense approach we take with Financial Freedom.

Gary Moore, our accountant and attorney, not only helped us with many of the technical questions but also was a tremendous source of encouragement. He often reminded us that a book like this could truly make a significant contribution to people's lives.

Our new friends at Rodale Press deserve special thanks. They educated us in the ins and outs of what it takes to turn a rough draft into a readable book. Jane Knutila was adventurous enough to participate in our weekend seminar and was transformed from art director to advocate. She did a fabulous job with the cover. Copy editor Susan Berg paid painstaking attention to detail to maintain the integrity of the manuscript, and Alice Feinstein provided the leadership that guided the editing process. And then there's our editor, David Epstein, who is in a class by himself. David taught us over and over how to translate what we wanted to say into something you would want to read. He threw himself heart and soul into this project and, for his efforts and talent, has our unending appreciation.

Mary Vaessen, our friend and assistant, nursed this project from its very beginning in 1985. Her organizing and editing enabled us to remember what was going on in each chapter.

John-Roger, our friend, colleague and teacher, continues to inspire us by demonstrating a true consciousness of wealth.

And last but certainly far from least, we want to thank the many who have participated in the Financial Freedom seminars over the years. They are the ones who helped us build a bridge uniting finances with psychology.

INTRODUCTION

THINK WEALTHY,
AND THE MONEY
FOLLOWS

Ninety percent of all people are afraid that they don't have enough money. And the other 10 percent are afraid of losing what they have.

This may sound unbelievable, but as psychologists who've counseled thousands of people about money, we know that the relationship between people and their money (or lack of it) is *not* about economics. Instead, we have discovered that *the state of your finances is really controlled by your state of mind and emotions.*

Just how powerful are our beliefs, thoughts and feelings about money?

Try this: It's been said that if we took all the money in the world and divided it evenly among all the people alive on the planet, each person would have over $1 million. However, within only ten years we'd all end up with the exact amount of money we have today.

Why? The answer lies with the *mind-set* of each of us. Without learning to change your attitude, you'll never be able to have a truly significant shift in your financial life.

But don't get the wrong idea. Your finances don't have to be a terrible burden. Believe it or not, they *can* be easy. Like anything else, your finances tend to deteriorate when neglected and to thrive when you give them attention.

In the early days of our counseling, we had some clients who helped us learn three invaluable lessons about people and their money. We'd like to tell you about Elizabeth, Charles and Lisa. They're all clients who learned to take charge of their financial lives, even though they seemed unlikely candidates for success with money. (Perhaps you can relate!)

THE HIGH PRICE OF DENIAL

Elizabeth, an attorney, rescheduled her first financial counseling session with us because she couldn't find her checkbook. Next she rescheduled her second appointment because she couldn't find her bank statement. When she called to reschedule her third appointment because she couldn't find her bills, we strongly suggested she simply show up empty-handed—*fast*. We'd never encountered a person with such an inability to find her financial papers. It didn't take Sherlock Holmes to realize that she had hidden reasons for her inability to provide us with detailed information about her financial practices. And we were right.

Elizabeth arrived in a state of anxiety. This, we quickly found out, was her chronic response to living a life in which her finances had gotten completely out of control. Here was an attorney who told us she didn't pay her bills because she couldn't find them!

We wondered what was *really* going on with Elizabeth. Attorneys don't just *lose* their phone bills month after month . . . not to mention their MasterCard bills.

During a counseling session in which we gained Elizabeth's trust, she finally told us that she was so frightened that she might be in debt, she didn't want to know the truth of her financial situation. No wonder she couldn't find her checkbook, bills and papers! From our perspective, this was a manifestation of Elizabeth not wanting to look at the state of her finances. Or as Elizabeth said, "I'm afraid to look at my money status. I figure if I ignore it, it'll go away."

Lesson 1: Some people are in complete denial about the state of their finances simply because they're afraid to look at the facts.

Elizabeth's heavy-duty resistance to becoming aware of her own financial situation was a sobering revelation to us. We wondered how many other people were opting for this painful denial of how much money they did—or didn't—have.

We got our surprising answer from a survey we did of several hundred people. A full 30 percent admitted they were unwilling to honestly look at their finances *because they didn't want to find out just how badly they were really doing.* (Imagine how many were too ashamed to honestly admit it!)

CHILDHOOD PATTERNS AND ADULT ANXIETY

Why was Elizabeth so frightened to look at her finances? From the information we'd been able to gather, we figured that even though she was totally disorganized and frightened, Elizabeth was probably not in debt. In fact, based on approximations of her salary and her probable expenses, we suspected that Elizabeth had several thousand dollars in her checking account that she was completely unaware of.

So why the overwhelming fear of debt? Answering this question would be the key to unlocking Elizabeth's denial.

At the start of one of our counseling sessions, we asked Elizabeth if she would be willing to explore the roots of her fear of being in debt.

She was.

Lesson 2: While denial is debilitating, the willingness to look at your financial situation will empower you.

Under our guidance, Elizabeth courageously faced her fear of debt, tracing it all the way back to her childhood.

When Elizabeth was young, her parents bought a farm. The farm was heavily mortgaged, and her family was always in debt.

Her father was an alcoholic. When he drank heavily, which was often, he'd have highly emotional scenes in front of his children. He'd cry that they were one step ahead of the poorhouse. He'd howl that they were about to lose everything and be tossed into the road penniless, with nowhere to go.

Through exposure to her father's anxieties, Elizabeth internalized a pattern of terrible fear of debt. She carried this psychological pattern with her into her adult life.

When it came to her finances, Elizabeth was an emotional hostage of her past. Her response to her childhood experience had determined what her future response to money would be: fear.

The ties that bind an emotional hostage can be very strong. In Elizabeth's case, for example, a grown woman was afraid to discover that she was a well-paid attorney with more than enough money to cover her expenses.

After Elizabeth confronted the source of her fear, her relationship with money totally changed. She became willing to take a careful look at her finances.

Over several counseling sessions, we waded through her checkbook, bank statements and bills. Together, we took on the important task of creating an accurate picture of Elizabeth's personal finances.

Why is this important?

Because the willingness to look provided Elizabeth with an opportunity to discover what *really* needed to be done about her finances. The same can be true for you.

In Elizabeth's case, she found out that she wasn't in debt after all. She was, however, spending almost all that she made—and not saving for her future. Her retirement fund? Zilch. And by not paying her bills on time, Elizabeth saw that she had racked up exorbitant late fees and interest charges. All this was in addition to the stress of never knowing from one day to another just how much money she really had.

By continuing our work together, we remedied all of Elizabeth's money troubles.

Now the little girl who was once frightened of debt is a successful attorney specializing in estate planning and financial counseling. Her favorite clients? People who are afraid to look at their finances because of what they'll see.

HOSTILITY, SELF-DECEPTION AND OTHER OBSTACLES TO SUCCESS

Charles, a successful Los Angeles Realtor, came to us for financial counseling and vowed he was serious about getting his finances turned around. He and his wife, Lisa, a graphic artist, were constantly spending beyond their means. As a result, both were suffering emotional upset and stress.

At the end of our first session, we asked Charles to bring their money management system to the next appointment. Charles's response was to tell us in no uncertain terms that they had a fine system, thank you, and that was not the problem. Furthermore, he had no intention of wasting time going over something that was already working for them.

Hmmm. A tad hostile and very defensive, we thought. We'd just have to smoke the reasons out into the open at the next counseling session.

"How are you preparing for the future?"

That's how we started our second meeting. "Are you putting away money for your retirement and your child's education?"

"Oh, sure," they replied.

"How much?" we asked.

Silence.

Then they hemmed and hawed a while, before admitting they didn't really know how much money they'd put away.

We explained that we really couldn't help them get their spending under control if we didn't know how they were apportioning their funds. We suggested that Charles reconsider bringing in their money management system.

He relented.

When he brought their "system" to our next meeting, we could tell at once why Charles and Lisa couldn't possibly get a handle on their finances.

What Charles saw as an "excellent system" we saw as a catastrophe!

Yes, it's true that he did have all their records, but they were simply in piles stored in shoe boxes, with no organization to them. He didn't even have a way of telling which bills were paid and which were not.

All along they'd been telling themselves that they had a gangbuster money management system, but the truth of the matter was that they didn't. In essence, they'd been lying to themselves about their money situation. And that is a dangerous thing to do.

Why?

In the case of Charles and Lisa, their "disinformation" precluded them from taking the necessary constructive action their finances called for. They really *needed* to sit down and create a money management system that worked for them. Instead, they told themselves their ineffective system worked just fine. And that was far from true.

The result?

Overspending instead of saving. And two really stressed-out people.

Lesson 3: An effective management system supports both wealth building and peace of mind.

Charles and Lisa have been working for two years now with the personal money management system that we helped them to design. We're happy to report that they no longer worry about going into debt. All their bills are now paid on time. Nobody calls them anymore from collection agencies looking for payment. They systematically save for their retirement and their child's education. And they accomplished something they never thought possible: They took their dream vacation—a three-week trip to France.

Oh! And Charles isn't the least bit hostile or defensive anymore. (Well, maybe just a little bit about his weight, but that's another story!)

THE UNEDUCATION OF OUR NATION

Elizabeth, Charles and Lisa are far from being any exception to a rule. Why? Because most people in this country receive very little—*if any*—formal education in how to manage money. Instead, you learn about money—and the rest of life's important lessons—almost exclusively by the example demonstrated by your parents.

And where did your parents learn about money? Probably *not* at Harvard Business School. Nor through private tutoring by John D. Rockefeller and J. Paul Getty. No, they learned through the example set by *their* parents. Can you guess where your grandparents learned about money? (Hint: It probably *wasn't* Harvard Business School!)

So it's no surprise to us that today many people find them-selves *needlessly* living from paycheck to paycheck, with little hope and lots of frustration that they'll ever become wealthy.

The good news is: *Your life doesn't have to be this way.*

That's right. Our research shows that it definitely is within your power to change your thoughts, beliefs and feelings about money and to learn the attitudes and practices that build wealth.

Best of all, you can do it in as little as *eight minutes a day.*

Just read on and see.

THE FINANCIAL FREEDOM LOGO

When we began counseling people about money, we soon realized that a large number of our clients had what we call a negative mind-set about money. When they thought at all about their finances, it was usually in terms of lack and unpleasantness. They didn't seem to be aware that they could choose to think about money in a positive and uplifting way. As Ralph Waldo Emerson said, "Money, which represents the prose of life, and which is hardly spoken of in parlors without an apology, is, in its effects and laws, as beautiful as roses."

We wanted to give our clients a positive picture designed to remind them every time they looked at it that money can be viewed in a positive way. What better representation of all we truly value than the heart? Thus, our logo developed as an image of the dollar sign within the shape of a heart. Notice that it's not a heart within a dollar sign but a dollar sign within a heart. This conveys the notion that money rightly used is in service to what we truly value and not the other way around.

Our hope is that every time you see this logo, it will remind you that money can indeed be experienced from the perspective of Emerson: " . . . as beautiful as roses."

Part
I

*"The simple truth is that financial success does not depend
on the markets, luck or even talent. It depends on
how you think about yourself way down deep in the
deepest recesses of your subconscious."*

—HOWARD RUFF

THE MONEY/MIND CONNECTION

MEET THE PRESIDENT
OF A MILLION-DOLLAR
COMPANY: YOU!

Would you believe you are already President and Owner of a million-dollar-plus company?

Oh . . . you don't know anything about your $1 million?

Well, consider this. If you began working at age 25 and continue until you are 65, and if your average income during that time is $33,000 per year (an approximate national median), your lifetime earnings will be exactly $1.32 million. Not bad!

Total years worked and annual income vary from person to person, of course, but the fact is that the average American *does* make more than $1 million over a lifetime. So in a very real sense you *do* own a million-dollar company.

And just what *kind* of company is it that you own? By nature, it's a money management company, and your job is to successfully manage the more than $1 million that you'll earn during your lifetime.

Since you're going to be dealing with such large amounts of money, one of the smartest things you can do is learn all you can about how money works. That way, you can be the most successful money manager possible.

LAUNCHING YOUR VERY OWN COMPANY

Let's begin by giving your company a name. If your name is Bob Hamilton, you might want to call your company Hamilton Enterprises, the Hamilton Financial Group or, if you're married, Hamilton and Hamilton. Not surprisingly, we call ours Financial Freedom Unlimited.

Choosing a name for your company is an important step. You want to have pride in your company and its name, and you want to be very clear that this is *your* company and that you intend to manage it wisely. So go ahead and write your company name in the space below.

_____

Now that your company has a name, write in your name below as President or Chief Executive Officer (CEO).

_____

President/CEO

Being the head of your own company is a nice feeling, isn't it? You're in charge of the money going through your hands, and the management of that money is both your responsibility and your golden opportunity.

As President, the very first thing you'll want to do is begin establishing some financial goals for your company and some guidelines for achieving those goals. You may not know this, but the primary goal of every business is the same—*to financially benefit the owners.* Many companies (most of those on the stock exchange, for example) are run by professional managers hired to benefit the owners or stockholders. However, since you're both Owner and Manager, you're in the enviable position of managing your own money to benefit yourself and your family. This is a powerful and responsible position!

How's Your Company Doing?

When developing your company's goals, a good place to start is figuring out where you currently stand financially. So let's see if we can find a rough way to evaluate how your company's doing.

Try asking yourself this question: "Can I sit down right now and write a check for $7,300 that will clear my bank?"

If you've been working ten years and you can't write that check, it means you haven't built cash resources in your million-dollar-plus company at the average rate of $2 a day. And if you can't write a good check for even $3,650, you haven't put aside even $1 per day.

Regardless of how much you have (or haven't) saved, the good news is that by the time you finish this book, you'll be well on your way to writing checks like these without worry.

Here's another way to get a handle on your company's current financial status. Let's say you've been plugging away at this financial game a little longer and you've been earning an average of $33,000 a year over a 20-year period. Consistently you've been putting $166.67 a month (or $2,000 a year) into savings. Let's also assume that you've invested those savings in a tax-deferred individual retirement account (IRA) at a compounded rate of 8 percent a year. As the table below indicates, you'd now have $98,845 in your account.

SAVINGS OVER TIME

Interest Rate	10 Years	20 Years	30 Years	40 Years
5%	$26,413	$ 69,438	$ 139,521	$ 253,679
8%	$31,291	$ 98,845	$ 244,692	$ 559,562
10%	$35,062	$126,005	$ 361,887	$ 973,704
12%	$39,309	$161,397	$ 540,582	$ 1,718,284
15%	$46,699	$235,620	$ 999,914	$ 4,091,908

Take a moment to think of how long you've been working and then consult the table above to see how your savings compare. Are you anywhere close?

If you continued saving at this rate for another 20 years, you'd have a tidy nest egg of $559,562. Not bad! And if you were able to invest your money at 10 percent, you'd would wind up with close to $1 million!

If your spouse is working, too, and is also saving $166.67 a month in an IRA, all the numbers in the savings table are doubled. That's a lot of financial potential! Small wonder that you need to begin managing your million-dollar company in the best way possible to maximize your success!

HOW'S EVERYBODY ELSE DOING?

It's obvious that the way to become wealthy—not counting inheritance or winning the lottery—is to build a relatively large surplus of savings. But did you ever wonder just how many people are actually building up a significant surplus?

The U.S. Social Security Administration wondered the same thing and did a study to find out. They wanted to know what happened *financially* to 100 average Americans over a 40-year period—starting when they entered the work force at age 25 and ending when they retired at 65.

Of those who survived, the study showed that when they retired:

- 1.5 percent were wealthy. They could do what they wanted when they wanted.
- 5.5 percent were secure. They could do much of what they wanted with planning.
- 4 percent had no savings and had to keep working to support themselves.
- 89 percent were dependent on relatives, friends or charity for their survival.

These figures can be seen in the graph on the opposite page.

When we saw these results, we were truly startled! To think that 93 out of every 100 Americans who reach age 65 might have little in the way of significant savings is *not* pleasant. We certainly don't want to turn 65 only to find ourselves dependent upon Social Security, welfare or generous relatives. We suspect you don't either.

The good news is, you don't have to! There's a great deal you can do for yourself and your family to dramatically increase your wealth while also enhancing the quality of your life. As a matter of fact, that's what this book is all about.

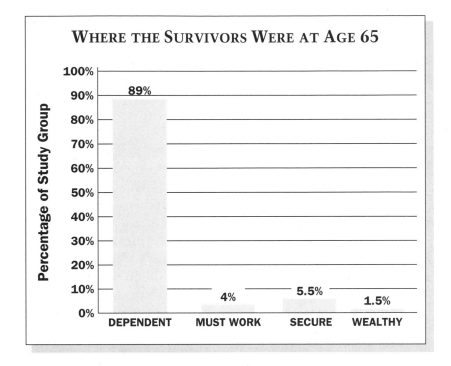

WHERE THE SURVIVORS WERE AT AGE 65

A SIGN OF THE TIMES

You're probably only too aware that in spite of what economists tell us about the low inflation rate, it seems to take more and more to buy less and less. Even if you're fortunate enough to have a steadily rising income, chances are you're challenged to stay even, much less increase your wealth.

During the past few decades, saving money has been deemphasized both individually and nationally. (That's certainly reflected in our country's current debt crisis.) At the same time, spending has been—and continues to be—encouraged by businesses wanting to sell you increasing numbers of goods and services.

At the same time, many people have grown used to living from paycheck to paycheck. They spend like it's going out of style. And eventually it does. For them.

That's exactly where Jack found himself when he moped into our office for his first counseling session. Jack had owned an electrical contracting business. At the ripe old age of 27, he employed 35 people and was well on his way to becoming a millionaire.

Only one thing stood in his way: his attitude about money.

Jack figured that since things were going so well, he would live life to the fullest. To him, it was very important to show his father how successful he was by spending money hand over fist. In fact, he was spending all he was earning and then some. After all, he told himself, the business is doing so well, he would simply "catch up" later.

Then the unexpected happened.

As the economy worsened and new construction declined, Jack's business fell further and further behind in paying its bills. In short, Jack, who was more concerned with impressing his father than with building wealth, mismanaged his business right into bankruptcy.

The hard part for Jack was having to fire his employees, many of whom had been extremely loyal. He knew their families and was well aware of the hardship this would create in their lives.

Worst of all, Jack had to move back home with his parents until he could recover financially. Rather than his usual habit of picking up the tab for family and friends at the best restaurants, Jack was now eating at home, where his folks could pay for the food.

Mostly he ate a lot of humble pie.

IS THIS A GLOBAL CRISIS?

Is Jack's self-destructive attitude of spend, spend, spend a particularly American approach to money? Or is there a Yoshi in Tokyo buying three Sony high-resolution TVs? A Johann in Berlin ordering his second custom-interior BMW? A Johnny in London being fitted for more tailored suits than he can ever wear?

The graph of savings rates on the opposite page shows how we, as Americans, recently compared with some of our developed neighbors around the world.

Many leading economists and financial advisers agree that the first order of business in anyone's financial life is to get out of debt and start saving. Yet studies show that Americans are saving *less* than at any time during the past half-century. As counselors, we're only too aware of how this affects people in everyday life. For example, many of our clients are couples seeking professional psychological help for relationship problems—made worse by money problems that have stressed these people to the breaking point.

Maurice is a businessman who earns a decent living for his

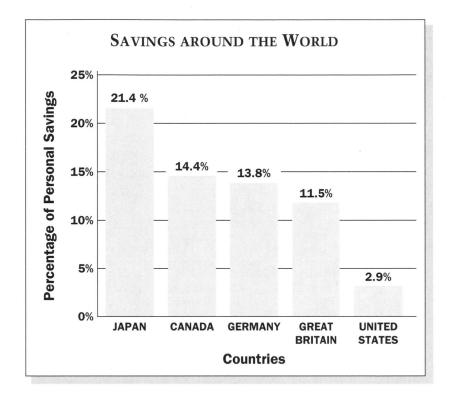

When it comes to saving for the future, how do Americans stack up? Not too well, it seems. Japanese and Canadian families save a far greater percentage of their income.

wife, Maggie, and their two children. By the time the couple came to see us, they were constantly fighting over money.

The problem? Maggie, who often helped Maurice by doing clerical work in his office, didn't like the way their money was being spent. She thought that instead of Maurice taking his clients to expensive lunches, he should hire her a housekeeper. That way, Maggie would be free not only to work in the office but also to take long-desired acting classes.

Maggie's position was that Maurice should pay her at least as much as he would pay someone he'd have to hire if she wasn't helping at the office. To her, the fact that he wouldn't showed her how little he really cared for her. She was angry and hurt.

Maurice's argument was that he'd love to be able to pay Maggie for her work. Better yet, he'd rather hire an office worker. That way, Maggie could be with the kids and even take acting classes, if that's what she wanted. However, they simply didn't have the income. And the fact that Maggie didn't acknowledge that Maurice was doing the best he knew how fed into his secret fear—all she saw in him was a meal ticket.

Worse news was yet to come.

When we asked about their savings plan, they told us they had none. In fact, as we began to piece together their finances, we found that they were spending more than Maurice was bringing in. Not counting the equity they'd accumulated in their home, they had nothing to show for their years of hard work and were, in fact, $50,000 in debt.

IS THERE A WAY OUT?

How did we assist Maurice and Maggie in turning around this potential disaster? One of the very first things we did was present five key concepts crucial to financial success.

We'd like to share these keys with you. Look them over, and as you do, assess your willingness to embark upon a remarkable journey that has the power to magically transform your finances and your life, just as it did for Maurice and Maggie.

1. Honest assessment. You must determine and write down exactly how much you're earning and spending right now as well as how much you owe.

The reason: To get where you want to go, it's essential to know where you're starting.

2. Future vision. Give yourself permission to dream and write down as clearly as you can exactly how you want your future to look regarding money, savings, security, investments and property.

The reason: Creating *anything*—including wealth—depends largely on your ability to focus on your goal. The clearer your goal, the more likely you are to attain it.

3. Specific goals. Setting short-, medium- and long-range financial goals is extremely important.

The reason: Short-term desires and longer-term aspirations are both important and must be in balance with each other for you to succeed. When goals are clearly identified, the creative part of your consciousness knows precisely what you want and has clear guidelines for attaining it.

4. Easy and effective tools. It's essential to have a simple structure and step-by-step methods, including clear directions and strategies, for both creating greater wealth and tracking your income and expenses.

The reason: The easier the process is to do, the more likely you are to do it.

5. Willingness to take action. When willingness is present, at least 90 percent of the work is already done.

The reason: Only consistent action over time is what produces results. And only *you* can supply the willingness.

Maurice and Maggie, we're pleased to say, were highly motivated and very willing to work with us, each other and themselves. They quickly realized that their mutual caring for each other was far deeper than their hurt feelings and disturbance about their debt.

Once they learned how to evaluate their finances and take constructive action together, most of their marital problems quickly cleared up along with their money problems.

Their million-dollar company was back on track!

THE CHALLENGE, THE OPPORTUNITY AND THE POWER TO CHANGE

We are well aware of how challenging it can be to build more positive financial habits. However, the alternative of maintaining the ones you currently have may simply be unacceptable. We think it's tremendously empowering to realize we can build new positive habits that have the potential of being rewarding not only financially but psychologically as well. In fact, there are people doing it every day.

To help you tap into your willingness to get started, we offer the following observation. There are two basic styles people use in relating to money: *Some spend 90 percent of their income and then look for a way to save the remaining 10 percent. Others save 10 percent of their income and then go about spending the remaining 90 percent.* (Usually the former are employed by the latter.)

The remainder of this book is designed to assist you in developing attitudes and strategies for getting your million-dollar company moving ahead in leaps and bounds! This is an opportunity to invest in yourself and your family for the rest of your lives! Every habit you presently have began sometime, and if you want new habits for yourself and your kids' tomorrows, the only appropriate time to begin building them is today.

CHAPTER
2

YOUR (VERY PERSONAL) RELATIONSHIP WITH MONEY

If you aren't an accountant or a financial analyst, you probably don't pay much attention to money itself. What probably concerns you most is your *relationship* with money: how much you have, don't have, owe and, probably most important, *want*—and how you *feel* when you're paying your bills.

In other words, the issue probably isn't those green pieces of paper with presidents on them but what you *think* about and how you feel when you've got a wad of them in your hand or when paying those bills.

Since we approach the entire question of money as psychologists and educators rather than as accountants, financial analysts or businesspeople, we tend to address it from an unusual angle—how your mind directly impacts your bottom line.

We've formulated seven fundamental questions that are essential to answer before you can begin to clarify **22** your relationship with money.

As you go through the questions, we suggest you answer them for yourself before you read what we have to say.

Q. What is money?

A. We always begin with this question because it's a recurring theme in all our lives. And it's very difficult to talk about something if you don't have a clear idea of what it is you're considering. We've all probably heard *money* defined as "a medium of exchange." That seems obvious. The more you have, the more you can exchange for goods and services.

But what is this stuff, really?

When we began researching the question, we found that some economists define *money* as a "store of value." If, for example, a gallon of gasoline costs $1.50, then the actual coins and pieces of paper totaling $1.50 would be equal in value to one gallon of gasoline.

In fact, this used to be true when money was actually backed by stores of gold and silver. At that time, you could take a dollar bill to the appropriate governmental agency and cash it in for an equal amount of silver. Dollars were even called silver certificates. Those words actually appeared on the bill. At that time, money was *truly* a store of value.

Today, however, our paper dollars are called Federal Reserve notes, backed only by our government's promise, printed on each bill, that "This note is legal tender for all debts, public and private." Now dollars are receipts for only a promise, not for precious metals.

What this means is governments can (and frequently do) change the rules about what money is worth. In fact, this phenomenon has been widespread. In its severest form, it's called hyperinflation. In Germany prior to World War II, people insisted on being paid daily because they knew their wages would be worth less the following day. In its milder form, it's called inflation, and it's happening in just about every country, including ours, every day.

This information made us realize we needed a universal definition of *money* that would hold true regardless of government uncertainty and economic conditions. We needed a definition that would be psychologically sound, that would make sense and that most everyone could accept. We also needed a definition that would offer a direction for how we might want to live our lives.

What we've come up with is this: *Money is the value we choose to place on our time.*

In other words, money is that portion of your life's limited and precious energy—otherwise known as time—that you choose to spend in exchange for particular goods and services.

For instance, if you earn $100 an hour and it costs you $500 for a quality suit, then that suit has cost you five hours of your life's precious energy. If you earn $50 an hour, that same suit has cost you ten hours of your life's precious energy.

Adopting this definition immediately puts money into a new perspective. It demands that you evaluate all your purchases in terms of *the amount of working time you'll spend* in exchange for what you're buying.

Think of it this way: Today's dollar bills aren't backed by precious metals (gold and silver); they're backed by precious energy (your lifetime, or *work* time, on earth). For us, this was an extremely empowering realization—one we still use to clarify the *real* value of many products and services we might buy.

Q. What are you working for?

A. Another way to ask this question is: If money is a means to an end, what is the end? What is important enough for you to give your life's precious energy to get it in return?

Obviously, there are basic survival needs—food, clothing, shelter—for which most of us are quite willing to trade our energy. Beyond that, purchases become a question of personal goals and values. Let's not kid ourselves—it would be wonderful to have an abundance of money so that we could buy whatever we'd like. But as Peggy Lee so knowingly sang, "Is that all there is, my friend?" While it would be presumptuous of us to tell anyone what he *should* be working for, we've found it very beneficial to help the people we counsel explore their many answers to the question "What *are* you working for?"

Our years of exploring the answer with thousands of clients have shown us a misconception held by many people—*they confuse standard of living with quality of life.*

When we talk about a standard of living, we usually mean how much money you regularly spend to support a particular lifestyle.

Generally, the more you spend, the higher your standard of living.

Of course, some people maintain a high standard of living by spending more than they earn. They do this by borrowing against future earnings—through abusive use of credit cards or other loans. And while the short-term effect can be a higher standard of living, the long-term result, unless corrective action is taken, will be debt and, ultimately, a lower standard of living *and* quality of life.

Quality of life is independent from standard of living. Although it's not a physical thing you can see and touch, a high quality of life is, for us, the true measure of wealth. It has to do with the richness of your life experience, including how you feel about yourself, how fulfilling your relationships with family and friends are, your level of integrity, the quality of meaning in your work, your self-respect and your self-esteem. All these can be positively experienced independent of your standard of living.

For us, the answer is that we're working primarily to enhance the quality of our lives so that we can spend our time doing more of what brings us fulfillment. And at the same time, we prefer enjoying a comfortable standard of living. This realization brings us to the third question—perhaps the most important of all.

Q. What activities truly bring you fulfillment?

A. From our years of counseling, we've found that most people find this question challenging. One very big reason: You may have been raised to think that your standard of living is your primary goal in life. Quality of life is then relegated to a by-product of "making it big."

To be fulfilled, you need to hold quality of life above standard of living. But it rarely occurs to many people that they can focus on quality of life as the *primary* goal and design their standard of living to support it.

To answer this question, ask yourself how you would spend your time if you could support your standard of living without needing to work. Once you start generating possibilities, ask yourself what it is about each activity that you like. In other words, "What is the quality of experience that I am seeking?" One of us (Ron) has a personal experience to relate in connection with this concept.

Years ago, I was working in a family business. It was a good business, I was doing well financially, and I knew that I would eventually own the entire company.

The problem was that I didn't enjoy what I was doing.

After about eight or nine years, it became clear to me that I needed to leave. I set a financial goal for myself and decided that once I had accumulated a certain amount of money, I would move on. I began saving, but as the months went by, I became more and more dissatisfied. I found myself regularly reevaluating my goal. The more I wanted to leave, the more willing I was to reduce the amount of money I thought I needed. Finally, one day I just decided that what I had was enough, and I left.

I learned three lessons from this experience. First, the greater the motivation, the more likely you are to achieve your goals. Second, in order to get what you want, it's often necessary to say no to what you don't want. And third, it makes a really big difference to be doing work that is meaningful to you.

In assisting people with financial planning, we find that it's not our job to judge whether someone else's goals are worthy. And it's not our job to say what experiences are fulfilling to you. However, what is essential is having goals that you think are important enough to motivate you to develop and stick with a sound financial plan that'll support you in achieving them.

When considering the question of what activities are fulfilling, some people decide to dramatically alter their standard of living. They're no longer willing to spend life's precious energy as freely as before. Instead, they want to accumulate more money.

This brings us to the next question.

Q. If you had lots of money, what would you do with it?

A. Would you wake up tomorrow morning and go to work, or would you take the marvelous vacation you've always wanted? What would you do next?

We had a friend named Bob who had a sailboat capable of ocean travel. He regularly sailed up and down the coast of southern California and dreamed of sailing to the Caribbean. One day he asked the owner of a sailing outfitter how long it would take to sail from Los Angeles to the Caribbean. When the owner told him, Bob asked about the return trip. The owner replied, "I don't know. No one has ever come back."

Having "lots" of money can be like that. Many people arrive at financial independence and "don't come back." Others feel inwardly that they have a mission and devote their lives to it. Again, it's not our intention to sit in judgment of what you choose. Rather, we're saying that in order for you to begin treating your million-dollar company more responsibly, it's important to have a plan for how you intend to use your financial resources. Research shows that those with clear financial goals *plus* a strong motivation to achieve them are much more likely to be successful. (We'll go into much greater detail about the underlying reasons for this when we discuss the process of creating wealth in Part III.)

Q. What's the difference between financial independence and Financial Freedom anyway?

A. When we began our own financial quest, we thought the name of the game was to accumulate our own tidy nest egg for retirement. But planning for retirement is one thing, and financial abundance here and now is something else!

When we speak of financial independence, we mean you can live on the interest generated from your savings and investments and you do not need to hold a job. To many, this sounds very attractive, and we have seen clients who are financially independent—and who also are bound by their money. They worry constantly about whether they have enough, about losing it, about having it taken away and about whether or not they could make it in this world without it. They frequently have concerns about whether the people around them are their true friends or are just attracted to their money. Although they possess significant material success, they are nevertheless living in lack because of their fears and focus, which reflect a consciousness of scarcity. Financial independence can be a blessing, or it can be a curse.

Financial Freedom, on the other hand, means that you have made peace with your finances, regardless of how great or small your wealth. It means you've learned how to live contentedly within your means. You have your desires and aspirations in balance, and you are always "going ahead"—that is, increasing your wealth.

Financial Freedom has nothing to do with how much or how little you have. Instead, this freedom reflects a consciousness of abundance, maturity and inner wealth. While financial independence is a function of how much money you have, Financial Freedom is a state of being.

And financial independence and Financial Freedom are by no means mutually exclusive. We know financially independent people who are also in balance and at peace with their wealth. They've learned how to manage their resources wisely and, in fact, often use significant portions of their money supporting philanthropic activity. And we know people who are financially free and have relatively little money. And what they have they share generously.

As we see it, why not go for both? We advocate being at peace with money, always increasing your wealth, as well as having financial abundance and prosperity right here and right now.

Q. What are your beliefs and attitudes about money?

A. As psychologists, we know only too well the vital role that beliefs and attitudes play in accomplishing any goal. More good intentions and great ideas are sacrificed because of limiting beliefs and negative attitudes than anything else we know. If you *believe* that you don't deserve $1 million or that you could never earn that much money, *the likelihood of your ever having it quickly goes to zero.*

Relatively little has been written about beliefs, attitudes and intention as they relate to the field of finances. Like everything else, there are healthy beliefs and attitudes (those that help you reach your goals) as well as unhealthy ones (those that hold you back).

The best thing about beliefs and attitudes is that they can easily be changed—more easily than people generally realize. While we may not have complete control over what happens to us in the physical world, we do, in fact, have the power to choose what beliefs, attitudes and thoughts we cultivate.

Perhaps the single most important thing you'll learn from this book is how to change your beliefs, attitudes and thoughts so that you can be more of what you want to be—including wealthy.

Q. Are there any "secrets" to getting rich, and if so, what are they?

A. The correct answer is a simple yes and no! There is no "secret society" we know of whose membership passes from generation to generation. There's no sure way to be born into a wealthy family and no secret method for winning the lottery. But there are guidelines or rules that seem to result in people getting wealthy. Not only are they in this book, we include clear instructions on how to follow them for maximum benefit. Here are the four we find most important.

Positive attitude. Perhaps the most important secret is that beliefs, attitudes and thoughts largely control what happens in your life and that you have complete and total dominion over what you choose to believe is true ("I *can* become wealthy in my lifetime").

Inner alignment. It's essential that your thoughts, feelings and behavior be in harmony with each other and consistently line up with your goals. This sense of "inner cooperation" will assist you in carrying out the steps that'll result in successful completion of your goals.

Determination and perseverance. You must be willing to consistently do what it takes to produce successful results, and you need to dedicate time to achieve these results. You must regularly commit some of your life's precious energy toward achieving your financial goals.

Responsibility. As we noted in the introduction, if we were to take all the wealth in the world and divide it equally among all the people who live here, within ten years it would all be right back to where it is now. The reasoning behind such a shocking statement is, in truth, psychologically valid. Since wealth is a function of consciousness, those not willing to take responsibility for their wealth tend to lose it.

Here's the real get-rich secret, for those with ears to hear: *Over and over, we've witnessed that wealth flows in the direction of those who know how to care for it.*

Before we go on, you may want to compare *your* answers to the seven questions we've raised in this chapter with our answers.

In the next chapter, you'll learn more about why the answers to these questions are an important indicator of how successful you'll be at building wealth.

CHAPTER 3

THE PSYCHOLOGY
OF MONEY

People attach strong feelings—both positive and negative—to money. Money is almost always emotionally loaded. It can carry with it feelings of love, satisfaction, power, freedom and security. Conversely, it often comes burdened with feelings of anxiety, fear, low self-esteem, powerlessness, victimization, shame and insecurity. The fact is, your early conditioning and personality determine what kind of feelings you attach to money, and those feelings can play havoc with your fiscal behavior, cash flow, bank balance and bottom line.

That's right, your personality can do more than just win friends and influence people. It can make you—or break you—at the bank.

When we say that your *personality* is controlling your purse strings, we're not talking about friendly smiles, warm handshakes and popularity contests. We mean that unique psychological complexity that's the storehouse of your behavioral and emotional traits. It's

30

the *me* Sinatra croons about in his lyric "I gotta be me." The *I* in Popeye's "I am what I am, and that's all that I am." The *you* in . . . well, uh, *you* know.

So how does all this fit together?

Well, the first thing to know is that your personality is composed of three interrelated levels of consciousness: the physical, the mental and the emotional.

THE PHYSICAL LEVEL

All your actions that involve money (or anything else, for that matter) take place on the *physical* level, which is like a theater stage where you live out the drama of your life.

The physical level includes your body, your relationships with other people, your career, your health and your finances. You *go* to work, you *earn* money, you *spend* money. These are all physical actions. They are things you "do" in physical world reality.

An important aspect of the physical level is that you have a certain degree of jurisdiction over what happens "out there" in your life. However, you rarely have anywhere near absolute control over what happens *to* you, since a great deal of physical activity involves other people, over whose behavior you have little or no influence. And while you do have some authority over what *you* choose to do, you probably find it hard to alter certain of your behavior patterns *even when you know they don't work for you.* (For example, take a look at your most recent list of New Year's resolutions. What happened to getting more exercise, eating right or giving up smoking and drinking?)

The point is this: *For most people, willpower alone usually isn't sufficient to change behavior.*

Why is it so difficult to alter certain behaviors? We'll address this question in much detail shortly. For now, it's important to know that behavior patterns *can* be changed—and that changing them can be challenging.

But don't lose hope—remember that 200 years ago, a trip from London to New York City was very demanding. Today, simply pack an overnight bag, buy plane tickets, and you're ready for the Concorde.

The good news: With what we know today, we can alter behavior patterns much more easily than ever before. This enhanced leverage comes with greater understanding of the workings of the mind and emotions—the underlying motivators of your behavior.

THE MENTAL LEVEL

Our thoughts, beliefs and attitudes are the stuff of the *mental* level. By thoughts, we mean both the ever-present chatter that's constantly going on in most people's heads as well as all the thinking involved in everyday decision making. It's essentially a dialogue going on in your mind. Some self-talk is actually good for you in that it is uplifting, reinforces your strengths and motivates you in becoming successful ("I deserve to be wealthy"). Psychologists refer to this type of inner dialogue as positive self-talk.

However, there's also negative self-talk. It tends to be judgmental and tells you all the reasons why something you want to do can't be done, isn't worth doing or is unavailable to you because of some personal defect, such as feelings of unworthiness ("I don't deserve to be wealthy").

What's important to know is that you *can* learn to direct your own self-talk. This is a critical step in empowering yourself to create more of what you want in your life, including money.

Your beliefs also influence your self-talk. They serve as a filter through which you define reality. We mean this literally—*what you believe to be true tends to be true for you, and what you believe to not be true tends to not be true for you.* Henry Ford is credited with first having said "Whether you believe you can or you can't, you're right." He understood the importance of beliefs in determining the course of our lives. Nowhere is this more clearly seen than in our financial lives. If you believe you can be wealthy, the likelihood of actually becoming wealthy is much greater than if you believe you cannot.

Here's an example of the power of beliefs to affect your financial life.

Peter was a successful surgeon. He came to us for counseling because he realized there must be some reason, other than bad luck, that he continued to lose money in his various investments.

It didn't take long to discover that Peter's problem was, believe it or not, a fear of disapproval.

Every time his broker called with a new "sure thing," Peter simply couldn't bring himself to say no. In a similar way, when an investment partner in an automotive repair shop wanted to buy a new piece of equipment, run a new advertisement or take a raise in pay, all Peter could answer was "Okay." He was literally taking money from his medical practice profits and just handing it over to his broker and his partner.

In Peter's case, this approval-seeking behavior stemmed from his early relationship with a very militaristic father, whom Peter believed it was *not* permissible to disobey. He'd been conditioned to believe that saying yes is the best way to get along in this world.

With Peter, our work consisted primarily of coaching him in recognizing and honoring *his own truth* while learning to be appropriately assertive. We also worked with him on learning to consider his self-worth as separate and independent from his willingness to agree or disagree with other people.

Peter had to change his core beliefs about what constitutes a healthy relationship. Happily, he sacrificed other people's opinions as the basis for the financial decisions in his business relationships. He found a place inside himself where he could be both a worthwhile person and someone who can say no. And has it saved him money!

Unlike the physical level, which at best is only partially under your control, the mental level is one of which you *can* consciously take charge. You have the power to think the thoughts you want to think and believe what you choose to believe.

If your beliefs are sabotaging you in experiencing the abundance, prosperity and riches you'd like out of life, you can choose to change them. We'll have lots more to say about how to do this a bit later. For now, know that you can choose the material that circulates in your mind in much the same way that you choose channels on your TV.

THE EMOTIONAL LEVEL

The *emotional* level consists of your feelings about people, things and situations. How you *feel* about your job, personal relationships, politics and the state of your finances is an emotional reaction to your thoughts, beliefs and expectations about situations that occur in physical world reality.

How can *what you tell yourself* affect your emotions?

As William Shakespeare wrote in Hamlet, "There is nothing

either good or bad, but thinking makes it so."

To understand this psychological dynamic, let's start with a definition of emotion. We like to think of the word *emotion* as "energy in motion." (Hats off to Einstein for explaining the physical universe with his law $E = mc^2$. But to navigate the tumultuous world of feelings, you'll do better to remember *this* law: E = NRG in motion.)

Energy, in its natural state, is neutral. In order for it to have a positive or negative "charge," you must associate it with particular thoughts or beliefs. That's why it's not unusual for the same event to trigger opposite emotions in different people. Individuals can have different beliefs about the meaning of an event. For instance, when the Soviet Union broke apart, people who believed that communism is an unworkable system celebrated. There were many people, however, who felt sad because they believed communism to be a superior system. Same event, different beliefs, different feelings.

Knowing this, we can further define *emotion* as "energy in motion triggered by thoughts and beliefs." Awareness of the relationship between feelings and thoughts opens a gateway in your quest for more positive beliefs and actions—not to mention a larger bank balance.

If you have negative feelings about your financial affairs, the first step to recovery is to be honest with yourself about what you're feeling. Are you angry, hurt, discouraged or perhaps fearful? Acknowledging and accepting these—and all other—feelings is critically important to reversing your current financial state. Why? Because your negative mental and emotional patterns are perpetuating your lack of money.

So what do you do about this?

Be honest with yourself.

When angry, hurt or fearful, most people feel better after expressing their upset, especially if they have a compassionate listener. (Our secret theory is that the best counselors in the world are *grandmothers*. Why? Because they listen to you with unconditional acceptance. A grandmother sits patiently and lets you cry your tears, all the while giving you the message that she still loves you and accepts you, no matter what. Imagine, she's got all that wisdom and no Ph.D.!)

And you don't have to depend on the presence of another person to reap the benefits of compassionate listening.

Consider this: If you respond well to being listened to by another, can you benefit from learning to listen more compassionately to yourself?

Our answer: Absolutely! We can't stress to you strongly enough how powerful and effective you'll become by learning to listen to your own feelings with an attitude of caring acceptance.

How do you create the proper atmosphere for listening to yourself? Well, for starters, think of the person who loves you the most. What is it about that individual that makes you feel so comfortable sharing *anything?* If you're like most people, it's because you feel *safe* with her. She never diminishes you for what you're feeling or hurts you by saying you're wrong or stupid or *anything* that belittles you. In essence, she *supports* you rather than *judges* you.

And that's the key—creating support rather than judgment inside yourself. One way to begin doing this: Think of your emotions as young children who need to be lovingly heard and understood—and who need nurturing, comforting and wise guidance.

With that kind of caring attitude, you can tenderly explore your emotions—unearthing whatever beliefs, thoughts, rules or standards you're holding in your mind that are the actual cause of your emotional upset.

The next step is to then reeducate your "emotional children"— those parts of yourself that experienced hurt, disappointment and misunderstanding in the past. By reeducating those parts through clearing up misunderstandings and limitations in thinking, you can reduce their contributions to emotional upset and financial limitation. Remember Elizabeth, the attorney who was afraid to look at her checkbook balance or pay her bills? She was an "emotional hostage" of her past, where she learned to strongly associate finances with fear. Through counseling, she was able to reeducate herself—by healing her childhood memories and learning to live, instead, in her prosperous present-day financial reality.

THE MENTAL GATEWAY TO WEALTH

If the situations themselves don't cause emotional reactions, what does? Of the three levels of consciousness we've just discussed, the mental level is by far the most important in determining what happens in the other two. As Abraham Lincoln once said, "I guess every man is about as happy as he decides to be."

There's nothing more valuable than the belief that you *can* reach a goal to help you accomplish it. And your emotions tend to line up with your beliefs—if you believe an event worthy of celebration, you'll tend to feel joyful and in a celebrating mood. Likewise, if you believe a tragedy has happened, you'll tend to feel sad. (Remember the different reactions of the Soviet people to the collapse of communism?)

By learning to intervene positively and strategically in your physical, mental and emotional levels, you can free yourself from barriers that keep you from opening up to greater wealth. Our goal is to assist you in learning how to change your behaviors and beliefs about money—all the while nurturing yourself emotionally. This *inner* progress will facilitate *outer* transformation—a life of ever-increasing wealth.

At this point in time, most of the people we counsel invariably ask us the following question (maybe it's on the tip of your tongue, too).

"Okay, Ron and Mary. I know I need to change my spending habits. And you're convincing me that I need to change how I think and feel about money. *But why is it so darn hard to do?*"

That's our cue to introduce people to their PALS.

PALS is an acronym for one of your mind's most important capacities—we call it your *Private Access Learning System.*

What does this system do that's so important?

It evaluates all incoming information trying to gain access to your mind—from the mundane "Go brush your teeth" to the complex "Am I worthy of being wealthy?"

This psychological system allows or denies "public access" to your thought center. Its prime directive is to protect you from making changes too easily that may adversely affect you.

This is a big job. Each piece of information is allowed access to the "private club" of your mind only after your PALS carefully evaluate it.

We like to imagine your PALS as a group of tirelessly devoted computer programmers. They man their workstations in front of a large bio-computer (your brain), on call 24 hours a day, every day of every year. Your PALS never take a vacation, nor do they ever rest. (Maybe they get some quiet time when you're asleep.) Regardless, your PALS are among your most essential inner workers—because they are completely devoted to your survival by *maintaining what has previously worked.*

The beliefs and behavioral patterns you've already learned have become ingrained as part of your personality, regardless of how effective—or dysfunctional—they may be. Since you've survived until now using these patterns and beliefs, your PALS won't allow them to be easily or radically changed—lest you court the possibility of some "unsurvivable" event. Generally, the longer a behavioral pattern has been in your consciousness as a core belief, the more challenging it's going to be to alter it.

From a survival point of view, this makes a lot of sense. Reluctance to change protects you from too quickly buying into something that's not in your best interests. This protection is often called healthy skepticism. When it comes to buying a used car, this dogged protection is great. However, from a personal growth point of view, this powerful reluctance to change makes it even more challenging to replace a dysfunctional or limiting habit pattern about money with another more empowering belief.

The good news: Habits are relatively easy to alter once you know how. What you need to do is clearly define which behavior you want to replace, identify the new behavior, line up your beliefs and feelings in harmony with the new behavior and begin doing it.

The bad news: Your PALS may find ways to sabotage your efforts to change. They want you to stick with what they know has previously worked for your protection and survival.

Here's an example of how this works.

Let's imagine that one day, you decide to start a brand-new program designed to help you get wealthy. (Sound familiar?) And let's say that as part of your program, you're instructed to gather together all your existing financial records (which we'll actually do a little later). Your PALS receive the instruction and go through an evaluation process that might sound like this.

Ooh! Isn't this interesting! Here's an instruction to begin gathering and organizing financial information 'cause this gal plans on getting rich. Hmmmm! This has gotta be a mistake.

We've never been asked to do anything like this before. All our previous instructions call for no particular systematic financial record keeping. Instead, we've been throwing things in a shoe box and waiting for tax time. It's worked for the past 15 years. We'd better deny access to this new request. It's just too different. Who knows what might happen? We'll file this instruction and input a behavioral command for her to have a cup of coffee and read the comics in the newspaper. If that doesn't make her forget about this new financial thing, we'll give her a command to go to the movies. That works every time!

And so it goes.

It's not that your PALS are purposefully trying to undermine your efforts. These "good friends" believe that running the new program isn't in your best interests, since it's contrary to the many previous instructions received from you about the lack of importance of record keeping.

So now we come to the heart of the challenge. The easy part is clarifying what to do differently. The demanding part is persevering and repeatedly reprogramming outdated beliefs and doing the new behavior long enough for your PALS to finally understand and accept the new beliefs and actions—and replace your old ones. This process of reeducation is accomplished over time. The length of time varies according to how effective and efficient a "change agent" you become in your own mind.

GETTING RICH WITH YOUR PALS

Psychologists generally agree that your future is largely determined by what you think and do in the present. Therefore, unless you're prepared to think and do something different than you've thought and done before, it's rather foolish to believe you can make any substantial changes in your life.

Since most new behavior begins with an *idea* that there's a better way to do something, the best place to begin getting rich is in *your mind.* We'll teach you to reprogram your thinking so that valuable new beliefs replace the old habits that no longer serve you financially.

Once you've learned how to program your mind for wealth, the next step is implementing new behaviors consistent with your new beliefs. If you're going to begin thinking like a wealthy person, you must begin acting like one, too.

So how will we work with your all-important PALS? In these four important ways.

1. Mental intervention. We'll help you identify your limiting beliefs about money and teach you how to change them into expansive beliefs. We'll show you how to replace negative self-talk with positive, affirming self-talk. This will assist you in sending clear messages to your PALS that you intend to positively transform your finances.

2. Physical intervention. We'll introduce a systematic set of specific, easy-to-follow steps to guide you through the Financial Freedom program. This new set of behaviors will positively reinforce the new instructions you're sending to your PALS.

3. Emotional intervention. We'll show you how to nurture yourself with the gentle support necessary for a positive learning experience.

4. Effective communication. We'll teach you to talk directly and effectively with your PALS to transform your relationship with money. Remember, your PALS are really in your corner. All they need is reassurance that you truly want to create more money. You'll provide this by demonstrating your willingness to change your beliefs and engage in new behaviors.

How long will this take? That's entirely up to you. But bear this in mind: You'll be making important changes—and they'll require time and effort on your part.

We believe you're worth it.

You are the President of a million-dollar company. Isn't it time to start acting more presidential?

Your first step can be to demonstrate your worth and value to yourself and your family by making the most important investment of your life—*the investment in yourself.* And please remember that although we're talking about money, the same process that works for money will also work to assist you in transforming any other area of your life—such as health, career and relationships.

In the next few chapters, we'll begin working with several powerful interventions to help you get started on your road to Financial Freedom.

CHAPTER
4

MONEY MYTHS THAT
STEAL YOUR WEALTH

Your beliefs about money are keeping you from the wealth you want and deserve.

Yes, it's true—your thoughts and beliefs about money are largely responsible for holding you back from achieving a financially abundant life. And there's a very good chance that they're also causing you tremendous stress and emotional upset.

But you're not alone—the same erroneous beliefs you may hold are so widespread that we think they're epidemic. They involve basic assumptions that you take for granted. Unfortunately, these assumptions function as self-fulfilling prophecies. We've found so many people with similar beliefs that we have developed a list of the most common Money Myths.

Our purpose in identifying these myths for you is simple. Once you recognize which of your beliefs are common Money Myths, you can replace them with more accurate beliefs. (Then you can issue new instructions to your Private Access Learning System, or PALS.) Eventually, you'll look at money in a whole new way.

Myth #1. Everything in my life would be wonderful if only I had more money coming in!

Reality. *More money coming in is usually accompanied by more money going out.*

In counseling individuals and families about their finances, we hear a recurring theme. Clients report taking abundance and prosperity seminars and then attempting to implement what they've learned. They tell us things like "I've been doing lots of affirmations and visualizations and techniques for programming success into my consciousness. I programmed for a better job, and I got the job. I'm earning more than I ever have before, and you know what? I still don't have anything tangible to show for it." The bottom line had remained the same.

The "mythological" approach assumes that if more money is coming in, you'll have more at the end of each month. However, money coming in (income) is only half the picture. What the mythology conveniently overlooks is the other half, which has to do with how much money is going out (expenses).

Time and time again we've found that an increase in income is simply matched by a similar increase in expenses. If you're used to cozy lamb's wool sweaters and you get a raise in pay, you somehow find yourself browsing in the super-cozy cashmere sweater department.

To understand why this phenomenon seems to work this way, we need only recall your PALS. Remember, their job is to protect you from making self-destructive changes too easily. For example, if your financial pattern is to live as well as you can while not going into debt, you'll find yourself spending all you earn and having nothing left at the end of each month.

Let's suppose you get a raise and have more money available. In order to maintain the status quo of having nothing left at the end of the month, your PALS will suggest more ways for you to spend money. Remember, they're not working against you. They're only doing their job, based on what you've previously learned.

Consider Ralph, a dentist we've worked with whose income had been increasing regularly. When he came to see us, he was earning $140,000 a year. He and his wife lived modestly. They had three children, whom they loved very much. They wanted the best education for their kids and decided to send them to private schools. Although these schools were expensive, Ralph and his wife felt it was well worth the money.

Over the years, their continual complaint was that they never seemed to have enough money to buy what they wanted. They couldn't understand it, considering Ralph's substantial income. Once Ralph's wife came to a session carrying a dining room chair to show us just how badly worn it was!

We sat down together and analyzed their financial position. When we added up all their yearly expenses, a step they'd never previously taken, they were shocked to find that the total was almost exactly $140,000. If they had continued this spending pattern, even with Ralph's relatively high income, they would have awakened at age 65 to find that, excluding the equity in their home, they had very little in the way of real resources. Happily, we can report that since they've implemented their Financial Freedom program, they now look forward to a prosperous future, complete with new dining room chairs!

Income and expenses need to be looked at *together* for either of them to make any sense. In the next few chapters, we'll show you how to work with them within the context of your overall financial plan.

Myth #2. Financial well-being is defined by either how much money I have or how much I earn.

Reality. *Financial well-being has to do with how much you keep of what you earn, how well you manage what you have and how soundly you sleep at night.*

In talking with people about money, their attitude tends to focus on the money itself, usually in terms of amounts. But think about it. It's not the money itself but what the money represents in terms of their security that bothers most people. It's when your security is threatened that you tend to become upset.

Barbara and Hank came to see us for counseling in an effort to resolve their marital problems. They told us of their high standard of living, and we noted that it seemed way out of proportion to their occupations. They explained that Hank had inherited close to $350,000. We asked them what kind of investment plan they had. They looked at us sheepishly and smiled. They had no plan. Neither of them had any training or guidance in money management. They simply had elevated their standard of living.

In two short years, they told us, not only had they spent all the money, but they were in debt as well. They had adapted to a certain standard and continued attempting to maintain it by borrowing, even when the money was gone. When we asked how they'd managed to spend so much in such a short period of time, Barbara nervously smiled and said, "We ate out a lot."

These desperate people were truly out of touch—with themselves, with each other and with their money.

Our work with them consisted largely of developing a plan for freeing them from some of their unhealthy spending habits and assisting them in getting out of debt as soon as possible. In their case, they'd waited too long to take constructive action and had to file for bankruptcy.

They also got divorced.

If you think Barbara and Hank are unique, think again. The fact is, they're not. Remember the graph on page 17—93 percent of the people reached age 65 with no significant resources to show for a lifetime of work. If they had saved just $2 a day for the 40 years most of them were employed, they would have been able to write a check for at least $29,200 and make it good. But most of them couldn't. Regardless of what they'd earned, they had spent almost all of it.

Myth #3. In an inflationary economy, using credit to create debt is healthy. It allows you to buy what you want now and pay it off later, when money will be worth less.

Reality. In most cases, debt is bondage and is best avoided like the plague.

So often we see people who have fallen into financial difficulty and have gone into debt. Since we wanted to better understand the nature of debt, we considered it in light of our new definition of *money* as "the value we choose to place on our time, our life's precious energy."

Since most people are familiar with a home mortgage, we'll use that as an example of how debt works. Let's say you want to buy a house but you haven't enough money to pay cash for it. So you go to a lending institution, make a down payment, borrow the remainder of the money to pay for the home and then pay off the mortgage to the bank over a set number of years. To do this, the bank charges a certain rate of interest determined by prevailing economic conditions. So far, so good. You get your home, the seller gets his money, and the bank charges you for the convenience of being able to buy the house now rather than saving up for 20 or 30 years. The government even encourages the practice by letting you deduct the interest you pay on your home from your income tax.

For many people, this is the sensible and practical way to finance a home, and lending institutions exist largely to fulfill this function. But you must remember and be clear about what it is you're doing. In effect, you're committing a certain percentage of your life's precious energy to paying back the mortgage every month for the next 20 or 30 years. If you earn $4,000 a month and your mortgage is $1,000 a month, you're committing to spending 25 percent of your life's precious energy to support your home. For most people, this is fine, and they're willing to do it.

In fact, this arrangement works so well that the practice has expanded to include not only homes but virtually anything else we might like to buy. It's called credit, and many people regularly use credit cards for this purpose.

Realizing you're actually *mortgaging your future* every time you use a credit card can be rather sobering when the bill arrives and you can't pay the balance. You are in effect saying that you're willing to spend some of your *future* life's precious energy on something you've just purchased.

It's when you charge more and more and go past the point where you have the resources to pay back the credit card company at the end of the month that you run into difficulty. When this happens, debt is the result. You have mortgaged your life's precious energy and are now committed to paying off not only the loan on what you've purchased but also additional high interest as well. In the example of a home mortgage, at least you have the physical property to show for your effort. If you're in debt, many of the things you've purchased with credit cards will be used up long before you've even paid for them.

To make the point even stronger, how would you like a risk-free investment that pays you between 12 and 20 percent tax-free? If you had such an investment, your bottom line would tend to grow very fast. These are the percentages almost all credit card companies charge you when the bill is not paid within the limits of the grace period (25 working days for most cards). And you pay these rates with after-tax dollars.

Consider this.

If you pay 12 percent interest on a credit card, 31 percent in federal income tax and 12 percent in state income tax, an investment would have to earn a staggering 34.6 percent in order to equal the savings you'd realize by paying down your credit card.

Is this how you want to spend your life's precious energy?

Our research clearly indicates that the people least likely to achieve financial independence are those who are living by spending up to the limit of their credit cards and then paying off the minimum allowed each month.

Why? It's simple—their PALS have been instructed that this is how they want to live their lives.

The good news: Your PALS are quite willing to implement a more effective way of dealing with finances. The non-supportive habit can be changed, and wealth building can proceed.

Here are three guidelines regarding the appropriate and inappropriate use of credit cards.

■ Pay off your credit card balance at the end of the grace period (when you receive your bill). If you can't do this, sincerely consider cutting up your credit cards until you can.

■ Avoid using credit cards to finance your standard of living. You're psychologically much better off if you temporarily lower your standard of living while you plan your strategies for increasing your income. This action doesn't have to lower your quality of life. In fact, for some people, it actually results in their improving it—they often learn to find more fulfilling (and less expensive) ways to spend their time.

■ Unless it's absolutely necessary, resist the temptation to use the "sky's the limit" line of credit, also known as the home equity loan. Yes, it's a loan at a lower rate of interest than what you pay for regular credit cards, but psychologically, it's unwise to finance your standard of living by agreeing to own less of your home.

If you sense that we're making a strong case for appropriate use of credit, you're right. Read on for why we feel so strongly. We have good reason.

Myth #4. Once I'm in debt, it's next to impossible to get out and become wealthy.

Reality. *Debt is like many other situations. It can be learned from and reversed.*

There are a variety of reasons why so many people today find themselves in debt, and some are very good reasons. Perhaps someone needed a loan to get through school. Maybe there was an illness in the family, and financial resources had to be used to care for the loved one.

All too often, however, many people simply live beyond their means by spending more than they earn.

If it were simply a matter of changing debt-producing behaviors, it might be relatively easy to obtain financial counseling and begin practicing new behaviors designed to get out of debt.

Unfortunately, as anyone who has ever had to deal with debt knows, it's not quite so simple. And the reason it's not so simple stems back to your friendly PALS.

Since your PALS' job is to protect you by maintaining previous habits, it follows psychologically that how *deeply* in debt you are is less important than how *long* you've been in debt. The shorter the length of time in any habit, the less ingrained it is, and the easier it is to shift. *But regardless of how deep or long you've been in debt, you can reverse the process and become wealthy.*

However, if you're in debt, you face two additional challenges.

The first—and more important—is the altering of your debt-producing habits. This takes place largely on the mental and physical levels. Mentally, you must learn to transform limiting beliefs into their positive counterparts. Physically, you must implement behaviors designed to line up *what you do* with *what you say you really want.*

The second challenge is the size of the debt itself. A question people often ask us after taking our seminar is "Assuming I follow your program and begin going ahead every month, is it better to take the surplus and invest it, or should I use it to pay down debt?" The strategy that seems to work for most people is a combination of investing part and using part to pay down debt.

From a practical point of view, it makes little sense to invest at 6 or 8 or even 10 percent when you can earn 12 to 20 percent by paying off credit card balances. On the other hand, the process of opening what we call a Wealth-Building Account and funding it with a portion of your income is an important positive reinforcement, directed toward your PALS, that you intend to increase your wealth. (We'll have more to say about your Wealth-Building Account in chapter 6, "A Quest for Balance.")

How to split the allocation between wealth building and debt reduction is an individual decision depending on what seems to suit your temperament best. Obviously, the more debt you can pay down each month, the sooner you'll be debt-free.

We have found that once people can squarely face their ever-increasing cycle of debt, they realize they *must* change. As one of our clients said, "I just can't keep doing my finances this way. It *doesn't* work." We've seen people willing to trade their standard of living for an enhanced quality of life.

Often they go through a process similar to what we see with people who give up alcohol or drugs (or any addictive behavior). It's as though the process of honestly facing debt and seeing what you've done to yourself and your family stirs a place of tremendous resolve inside—which transforms your habits instantly.

Our point is that anything, even debt, can be used as a vehicle to turn your life onto a track more to your liking.

The most important thing to keep in mind about debt is that you can eliminate it very effectively using the information and tools we're providing in this book.

Myth #5. Financial success is an economic event. It has to do with what you know, who you know and how lucky you are.

Reality. Financial success is largely the result of several related psychological processes.

In chapter 2, "Your (Very Personal) Relationship with Money," we defined *money* as "the way you choose to spend your life's precious energy." We suggested seriously considering spending your energy seeking enhanced levels of fulfillment rather than simply raising your standard of living. Accepting this line of reasoning requires a redefinition of *financial success* as "maintaining the standard of living that supports you in living a fulfilling life and doing more of those things that are meaningful to you."

Ralph, our dentist friend who was earning $140,000 a year, was also spending $140,000 a year. Part of his idea of "living a fulfilling life" meant having savings available so that his children could go to good colleges. It also included saving for his retirement. These needs were not being met. The more he earned, the more it seemed to cost his family just to maintain what it had. There was no going ahead.

We've observed this pattern many times. Your PALS do an excellent job of maintaining the status quo in service to protecting you. This is why people resist change. We tend to be comfortable with what's familiar. Some psychologists refer to this as a "comfort zone." Once a habit, good or bad, is programmed into our consciousness, it tends to remain there until other programming replaces it because it is both comfortable and comforting. It's what we're used to.

For the dentist and his wife, change meant educating them regarding the philosophy and practice of Financial Freedom and then supporting them over time while they learned to do it. For the couple who had spent their inheritance, it meant a drastic change in lifestyle. For some, it may mean going to organizations like Consumer Credit Counseling Service or Debtors Anonymous for assistance.

This is why we are so strongly opposed to the inappropriate use of credit cards and why those who spend up to the limit of their cards and pay the minimum balance are the least likely to achieve financial success. This type of behavior, over time, trains you that this is the way you want things to be. You're literally programming your PALS into a habit of debt just the same as you would program in a smoking habit or an alcohol habit. And nonsupportive habits all have one thing in common—they erode self-esteem and self-confidence and make it very difficult to feel worthy enough to achieve the goal of living a fulfilling life. Building sound financial habits, on the other hand, tends to result in greater self-esteem in addition to enhanced financial well-being.

As you read through the remainder of this book, we'll be sharing with you the keys and tools we've developed specifically for working effectively in this arena. We'll also be assisting you in developing your own Financial Freedom program, tailored to your needs.

Maybe you'll find this challenging, or perhaps you'll find it easy. Whichever way it is for you, you'll succeed if you persist—because the pattern you start today will become the habit you live tomorrow.

In the next chapter, we'll begin assisting you in identifying and positively transforming your personal Money Myths.

CHAPTER
5

Transforming
Your Personal
Money Myths

Much of what you take for granted as "true" you learned from your parents or teachers when you were very young.

"Big boys don't cry."

"Never talk to strangers."

"Always keep your legs crossed."

In our counseling sessions, we've found that people are genuinely surprised when they begin questioning some of their beliefs. Once they look at these "truths" in light of real-life experience, many people find their beliefs are not as true as they once believed. This can be particularly so with beliefs about money.

To achieve Financial Freedom, you must identify the Money Myths that are part of your belief system.

Let's take a few minutes right now to identify some of the personal myths that may be hampering your efforts to become wealthy. You may be held hostage by them and not even know it. In our experience, most people are. How can you tell if you're one of them? We suggest that you respond to each of the following 30 statements by writing a T (true) or an F (false) in the space provided. It's important that you trust your first impression, and remember that your answer isn't right or wrong, only *honest.*

Please complete this test before reading any further.

_____ 1. I have to work hard doing something I don't enjoy to make money.

_____ 2. If I create more wealth than my parents did, I'll make them look bad. Good children don't achieve more success than their parents.

_____ 3. If I were better educated, I'd have the training and credentials needed to make more money.

_____ 4. If I had chosen a more lucrative profession, then I'd have more money.

_____ 5. If the economy were better, I'd make more money.

_____ 6. If only I'd had better breaks, then I would be wealthy. Other people have had more opportunities than I've had.

_____ 7. If my parents had been rich, I would have learned how to make more money.

_____ 8. I need to be in the right place at the right time to make any significant money.

_____ 9. If my boss appreciated me, then I'd get promoted and make more money.

_____10. If I didn't have all these family responsibilities, it would be easy for me to pay all my bills and live debt-free.

_____11. Enjoying money is not a good thing. It's a reflection of greed and selfishness.

_____12. I am so far in debt that I can never get out.

_____13. I can't do the things I want in life because I don't have enough money.

_____14. If I create great abundance and prosperity for myself, then I'm hoarding resources and depriving others of their fair share.

____15. There's never enough for me to get the things I really want.

____16. There is not enough for everybody. Some people have to do without.

____17. If I had a lot of money, other people would resent me and/or try to take advantage of me.

____18. If I had a lot of money, I couldn't handle the responsibility. I'm not good with numbers.

____19. To make a lot of money, you have to be dishonest and do illegal things.

____20. I'd feel guilty if I were one of the idle rich. I must work hard to prove that I'm worthwhile.

____21. If I want something, I just buy it on credit. I can have whatever I want now and just pay it off over time.

____22. If only I had a business of my own, where I'd be the boss, I'd have all the time and money I want.

____23. If I were more talented, I'd have more money.

____24. Meeting the "right people" would open the doors to financial abundance for me.

____25. Making money is a matter of luck.

____26. I'm unworthy of the "good" things in life, including financial abundance.

____27. Staying out of debt means I'd have to rigidly discipline and deprive myself.

____28. Wealth is a sign of materialism rather than spirituality.

____29. Wanting to have more money is a sign of greed and selfishness. I'd rather be pure and poor.

____30. With my money history and family background, it's impossible for me to get ahead.

How did you do? Some true and some false? Now you're probably wondering where the "answers" are.

Well, you can stop looking for them, because in our opinion, there aren't any answers. This doesn't mean that there's nothing to learn from taking this test. As a matter of fact, we think it's extremely valuable. Why? Because rather than puzzling over which answers are true and which are false, what you really want to know is which beliefs are working *for* and which are working *against* your becoming wealthy.

That's right. If you answered "true" to *any* of the statements on the test, congratulate yourself. You've successfully uncovered some of your personal Money Myths, which are undermining your efforts to become wealthy.

"What?" you might cry in amazement. "How can this be? They sure seem to be at least partially right to me."

More congratulations! You've stumbled upon a major obstacle many people have to becoming wealthy—a reluctance to look at "what is" because of not wanting to be "wrong."

Many of us have associations stemming from early childhood that being "wrong" is the same as being "bad." *This single psychological dynamic is responsible for stopping more people in moving forward in their lives than anything else we know.* All of us have learned to protect ourselves because we always want to be "right." Fear of making a mistake—or playing it safe—is the predominant reason most of us stay where we are. Moving ahead means taking risks, and taking risks means making a fair share of mistakes. Too often we fear mistakes—being "wrong"—and protect ourselves by not taking risks. But no risks means no mistakes, and no mistakes means no learning! It's as simple as that.

You may ask, "What about all the years of experience I've had? Doesn't that count as learning?" Well, it depends upon what you mean by "learning." We're reminded of the salesman who went for a job interview. When he didn't get the job, he was a bit angry and said to the interviewer "I know how to sell. I've had over 20 years experience at selling."

The interviewer replied, "I'm sorry, sir, but from your performance records, it seems more like you've had one year's experience 20 times."

Contrast him with the salesman who went for a job interview at a company where the interviewer actually administered an ink blot test to each applicant. When the interviewer poured ink on a piece of paper, the salesman inquired whether she did this for each job applicant. When told that she did, the salesman immediately began a pitch for a line of ink he said would work better than the one she was using. He demonstrated an ability to perceive the sales opportunity present, took a risk and—not surprisingly—got the job!

THE TRICK THAT UNLOCKS THE DOOR TO WEALTH

Remember what we said about the importance of being willing to make mistakes in order to learn? Let's take a look at some of your personal Money Myths. What if you consider them simply as misunderstandings that you bought into as you grew up? You now have an opportunity to clear up these misunderstandings and learn more effective beliefs. And this is where you can learn to successfully overcome any fear you have of making mistakes. How?

The trick is to separate making mistakes from being "wrong" or being "bad." Using this one key will do more to unlock the doors of wealth than any technique we know.

How do you accomplish this? It's really very simple! Success requires redefining reality so that anything you do with money has nothing to do with right or wrong, good or bad. When you make mistakes, a winning attitude is one of "I simply made a mistake. Now let's see what I can learn from it—and how I can use my learning so that I can be more effective next time."

Recognize that you're human, and care enough about yourself to dare to take risks, make mistakes and learn.

An extensive survey of elderly people revealed the single most reported regret was "I wish I had taken more risks and tried more new things." Making mistakes is part of life, and learning from mistakes is a hallmark of success.

So now let's look at some of the statements you answered "true" and see how to use them in service to learning and increasing your wealth. As an example, let's consider the third statement on the test: "If I were better educated, I'd have the training and credentials needed to make more money."

Many people believe this is true and blame their lack of success on it. Let's first consider the degree of "truth" in the statement itself. While statistics do indicate that greater levels of education and training are frequently associated with higher levels of economic success, it's equally true that many multimillionaires have less than a high school education.

And while education and training can often result in financial success, it's *not true* that unless you have the education, you *cannot* succeed. In fact, most—if not all—successful people say that attributes such as initiative and ability to effectively relate with others are *far more important than level of education in determining success.*

WHAT'S GOING ON IN YOUR MIND?

Now putting aside any discussion about whether the statement is true or false, let's turn our attention to how the statement itself operates in a person's consciousness.

If you believe you can't make more money without additional education and credentials, a good idea might be to acknowledge your desire to better yourself financially and investigate the possibility of getting more education or training as a way of getting a better job. What's more likely is that you use the belief as a justification for not taking action in support of yourself and for limiting yourself.

Why is this so? For the answer, you need to look only as far as your Private Access Learning System (PALS). Since your PALS' job is to protect you by maintaining the status quo, any action you might take to *change* things will tend to trigger a "We'd better not do that" response from your PALS.

One of the methods your PALS use to keep things as they are is to utilize your belief patterns as justification for *not* taking action. The reasoning goes something like this.

> *Since I have to be better educated to get a better job and earn more money—and since I don't have the time or the resources to become better educated—there's no point in even thinking about becoming wealthy. So I'll just stay where I am—where it's familiar and safe. After all, I can't earn more money because I'm not better educated.*

And on and on it goes, with each round reinforcing the round that went before—and thereby reinforcing the belief. By now the pattern is operating more or less automatically and is what psychologists call a self-fulfilling prophecy. And of course, the more this pattern becomes ingrained in your consciousness, the less likely you are to actually go after the education you think you need.

FACING FEAR OF ENVY

Let's look at another one. Statement 17 says: "If I had a lot of money, other people would resent me and/or try to take advantage of me." Again, begin by considering how true this may be. While it's true that some people resent those who have more than they have—it's called envy—other people love to see those they know get ahead in leaps and bounds. They figure that if you can do it, so can they—it's called inspiration.

Now let's look at how this statement operates in your consciousness. To the degree that you believe this statement, your PALS will talk to you like this.

> *If other people resent you for how much you have and try to take advantage of you, you'll have to spend all your time watching out for them. And since you'll never know who likes you for you and who likes you for your money, you won't have real friends you can count on. You'll be lonely or, worse, surrounded by people who are interested only in your money. It's much better to stay where you are and to not try to get a lot of money. It's just not worth it.*

Can you see how once again, to the degree that you believe this to be true, the likelihood of your being willing to learn how to draw more money to yourself diminishes?

In exactly the same way, each of the statements in the true/false test has a degree of truth in it but is not the whole truth. And regardless of the degree of truth inherent in the statement, the negative aspects of each statement are what you remember. And this negativity makes it less likely that you'll take action, which in turn prevents you from altering your beliefs. It's no wonder that most people find it very difficult to change their behavior.

Thankfully, the way out of this situation comes from knowing how to work with your PALS effectively. Initially, when you were very young, you didn't have the ability to intelligently evaluate what you were learning. So you learned many things, some of which limit you to this day and some of which assist you in expanding and growing. Now, as an adult, you're more sure of what you want. What you need to do is to let your PALS know this— they're open to your needs and aspirations changing. They'll run whatever program you choose to play in your consciousness once they're assured that the program is in harmony with their job of protecting you. Only now some *time* will be required—long enough for your PALS to become convinced of your intention to become wealthy and accept it as the new directive.

You can begin by looking at each of the statements that you marked "true." Ask yourself how much of the statement is really true for you (for example, "I don't have the education to become rich"). Then you look at the behavior that tends to result from the belief ("I don't try to better myself; I act like I've given up on becoming wealthy"). If you want to change your belief, write down the "realistic" statement ("While education may be helpful, it's not critical to my success. My initiative and ability to communicate with people are far more important than my education. And if I want more education, I can get it"). Begin saying this to yourself over and over until you believe it. When you're absolutely certain you believe the new statement, the likelihood is that your PALS have accepted the new belief as true and that you'll no longer be limited by the old belief.

How long will this process take? The length of time varies according to how much you really believe the old, limiting beliefs, how often you're willing to tell yourself the new beliefs and how flexible you are in working with yourself.

And remember, the more often you engage in the process, the faster you will see results. If you want to begin changing how much money you have, this is the place to begin. In our experience with counseling people, it's rare that anyone changes any behavior without first changing his beliefs about the situation.

There's a famous biblical quote that says "As a man thinketh, in his heart he becomes." We'd like to paraphrase it to capture the spirit of getting wealthy: "As a man thinketh, in his purse he becomes."

To assist you in implementing your Financial Freedom program, many of the chapters, beginning here, conclude with specific Action Steps. They summarize the key information and lay

MENTAL TIP ▚▚▚▚▚▚▚▚▚▚▚▚▚▚▚▚▚▚▚▚▚▚▚▚▚

An especially powerful way of transforming your Money Myths is by saying your new beliefs out loud while looking into your own eyes in a mirror. This gives you direct and immediate access to your PALS. If you want to experience how powerful this can be, go to a mirror right now and try it.

▲▼▲▼▲▼▲▼▲▼▲▼▲▼▲▼▲▼▲▼▲▼▲▼▲▼▲▼▲▼▲▼▲▼▲▼

out a systematic approach designed to produce certain results. In this chapter, the result is beginning to positively transform your personal Money Myths.

ACTION STEPS ~~~~~~~~~~~~~~~~~~~~~~~~~~

1. Identify what it is about each true/false statement that makes it seem true to you.

2. Look at the behavior that results from believing the statement.

3. Challenge the "truth" of the statement by asking yourself if you really believe this. It might be something you "picked up" along life's way that really doesn't square with your current, updated point of view.

4. Write down a more "realistic" statement (which you can recognize by its opening up new choices for behavior).

5. Repeat the new statement until you're certain you believe it completely.

6. Congratulate yourself for your willingness to transform your personal Money Myths.

CHAPTER
6

A QUEST
FOR BALANCE

Our definition of *Financial Freedom* is simple and to the point: having significantly more money coming in every month than is going out.

To achieve this, we need to explore several relationships, including those between income and expenses, desires and aspirations and creating wealth and tracking it.

Financial relationships, like other relationships, are something like a teeter-totter. When both ends are in balance, it takes just a little pressure to move the entire board up or down. If one end is very much heavier than the other, it may take a great deal of effort to bring them into balance. With finances, for example, it makes little sense to talk about income without discussing expenses. So let's start there.

INCOME AND EXPENSES

It's absolutely essential for you to understand the relationship between your income and your expenses.

Why? So you can learn to successfully leverage that relationship in your favor. When your income is greater than your expenses, the result is the accumulation of wealth. When your expenses exceed your income, the result is debt. If income and expenses are the same, your bills will be paid, but you won't be increasing your wealth.

Consider the state of your finances right now. Do you have significantly more money coming in every month than going out? Perhaps you do, and perhaps you don't. What's important is recognizing that whatever your behaviors and attitudes are right now concerning money, these are the habits *you've* built into your consciousness—and these are the habits your Private Access Learning System (PALS) will work to maintain.

The most important money habit for you to identify is the one at work in your relationship between income and expenses. This is why we say that financial well-being has less to do with how much you earn and more to do with *how much of what you earn you keep.* By "keep," we simply mean that portion of your income that each month you place in a separate bank account as your investment in your financial well-being.

We call your separate account a Wealth-Building Account. It's an extremely important part of your Financial Freedom program. It's the place where you accumulate your *gelt,* as Grandpa Hulnick used to say. *And we really do strongly suggest it be a separate account.*

Why?

For two reasons. First, when you're working to establish new mental and physical habits, you don't want to run the risk of your increased wealth getting mixed up with other funds, where it may be spent unconsciously. Second, the very fact that you have a Wealth-Building Account sends an unmistakable message to your PALS: "I wanna be rich"—as the upbeat dance hit affirms.

The money in your Wealth-Building Account acts like a seed. You want to plant the seed, nurture it, invest it wisely and watch it grow. In time, it'll become a full-grown money tree, bearing the fruits of abundance, prosperity and riches. They're your vehicle taking you toward financial independence.

When we talk about the value of saving a portion of income, some people react as if they were being asked to take a terrible-tasting medicine. We like to look at saving money from a more positive point of view. Since you and your family are the most important people in your life, you're really demonstrating your caring by investing in the future of those you love. We consider saving money to be an act of love and caring.

A valid question people often ask is "How much is a significant portion to be investing in myself and my family?" The time-honored approach among highly regarded financial theorists is setting aside *10 percent of your income* before paying anything to anyone else. We know people who place as much as 50 percent of their income in their Wealth-Building Account. Often these folks have financial independence as their major goal, and they figure that the more they invest each month, the faster they'll achieve it. What's our recommendation? After more than 20 years of counseling thousands of clients, we've consistently seen people make great strides by adding 10 percent of their income to their Wealth-Building Account each month.

You'll want to keep this store of money safe and carefully track how it grows. Watching this personal fund grow will reflect back to you your ability to create wealth and will actually act as a "magnet," attracting more money to you. The reason for this attraction is simple. By consistently saving at least 10 percent of your income every month, you're programming this new pattern into your consciousness and reeducating your PALS. This is how the new behavior pattern is accepted and established. The important thing is saving at least 10 percent of your income *consistently.*

Are we suggesting saving 10 percent before or after taxes? By saving 10 percent before taxes, your wealth will grow faster, but saving 10 percent after taxes is a fine place to start. It's a question not so much of how much you pay yourself and your family but rather of *consistently conditioning your PALS with the new, positive habit.* It's better to start with 1 or 2 percent and work your way slowly to 10 percent or more than to start with 10 percent and find out you need to keep dipping into it to pay bills. The first way builds the habit of increasing your wealth. The second way erodes wealth—and self-esteem along with it.

As a matter of fact, the best definition of *insanity* we've ever heard is "doing the same thing over and over while expecting a different result." Obviously, if you don't do something different, nothing is going to change. So if you want to become wealthy, you must act and think about money differently than you have been. Otherwise, it's very likely that your future will look exactly the same as your life looks right now. If your goal is more money, you've got only three ways to get there: You can earn more so that your income is higher than your expenses; you can spend less so that your expenses are lower than your income; or you can do both.

Approach #1. Increase your income.

Approach #2. Decrease your expenses.

Approach #3. Increase your income *and* decrease your expenses.

Let's consider the leverage available from relatively small changes. Say you follow Approach #1 or #2. You either increase your income by $200 a month or decrease expenses by $200 a month. If you were to place that $200 into tax-free savings each month and invest it at a compounded rate of 8 percent, at the end of 20 years you would have accumulated over $100,000.

If you use Approach #3 and increase your income by $200 a month while also decreasing your expenses by $200 each month, that would net you an increase of $400 per month. Assuming the same rate of return, you would have over $200,000 at the end of 20 years.

Suppose you would have been doing this for the past 20 years. Would the $200,000 you would have saved come in handy today? The stronger you answer yes, the more you need to learn the skills of the Financial Freedom approach to personal finances. The time is *now* for you to learn how to reeducate your PALS about the beneficial relationship between income and expenses so that you can increase your wealth as soon as possible.

DESIRES AND ASPIRATIONS

Many people think of income as the most important factor affecting their finances. However, as we've said, it's really the *relationship* between income and expenses that's crucial. Expenses are at least as important, and perhaps even more significant, a factor. So let's take a moment to look at the nature of expenses. We've found it useful to divide expenses into two categories: *desires* and *aspirations.*

Desires are short-term goals. They're all those things you want to have right now. They can range from an ice cream cone or a new shirt to new furniture or a new car. You're constantly bombarded with advertising to purchase these products and encouraged to buy them *now* because of some "great deal" that, if you hesitate, you'll lose forever.

Desires are usually emotionally based. They're almost always associated with the words "I want." Yet they can never be completely satisfied. For example, if you're driving a used car, you'd probably like a new car. When you get the new car, then before too long, you'll very likely want a new luxury car. And once you have your luxury car, what about an additional vehicle—a jaunty sports car or a private jet or yacht?

There's no end to the things you could buy if only you had a little more money . . . and yet a little more money . . . and still just a little more money. Psychologically, it's critical to recognize that because desires are largely emotionally based, at best they can be only temporarily satisfied. New ones *will* continually appear. There's no good or bad in this information—constant desires are simply indicative of the nature of how things are down here on earth. What is required, however, is learning a psychologically sound approach to working effectively with desires.

Aspirations, on the other hand, are based on deeply held values. They can be thought of as medium- and long-range goals. They're the things we'd like to have that usually cost considerably more than we readily have available. They include items such as a home, college tuition, retirement and, ultimately, financial independence. (When was the last time you saw a "heavy hype" advertisement for these products?)

And so the challenge is set in motion. You know it will be to your advantage to increase your wealth, thereby enhancing your quality of life. However, you're constantly challenged by your current habits, emotionally based desires and tremendous advertising pressure to spend up to and, indeed, past financially sound limits. What's a person to do?

It's important to keep in mind that *both desires and aspirations translate into expenses.* The only difference is that desires are immediate and aspirations are long-term. Psychologically, the relationship between them is much more important than how much money you make. If your desires outweigh your aspirations, you'll spend all you earn and perhaps even more. If your aspirations far outweigh your desires, you could find yourself in miserly deprivation while you hoard your wealth for a so-called rainy day.

As with income and expenses, you can learn to balance your desires and aspirations. What you choose to spend your money on is determined not solely by how much you have but also by what you value. The key is carefully choosing what you value, keeping in mind that while you can satisfy some of your desires, it's simply impossible to satisfy all of them.

If you're going to realize any of your aspirations, it's essential to learn how to psychologically balance them with your desires so that, regardless of your income, you save—not spend—a significant portion as an investment in your long-terms dreams (not the least of which may be financial independence).

Once your desires and aspirations are in balance, you're much more likely to enjoy life, secure in knowing that you're always going ahead, caring for yourself and your family first and maintaining a standard of living that supports the quality of life you've chosen.

CREATING AND TRACKING

The last relationship we want to consider doesn't have to do with finances in particular but rather is a relationship found in the structure of consciousness. We find consciousness involved with two essential functions that, when working in harmony, are quite capable of producing some fantastic results. When they work at cross-purposes, however, the results are like a tug-of-war. We call these functions *creating* and *tracking*, and once again, it's the balance between them that enables us to live most effectively and to consistently increase our wealth. Let's look at how they work.

Imagine you're building a house. First you design it according to your taste, while keeping in mind restrictions such as budget, lot size and local zoning laws. This part of the process is complete when your architect delivers a finished set of plans to you. To this point, you've been engaged primarily in creating.

Your next step involves hiring a building contractor, and then the work begins. It's the contractor's job to order the appropriate type and amount of building materials and to see that the structure is built according to your plans. Imagine what would happen if the contractor didn't know how many bricks, roof shingles or plumbing fixtures to order.

And worse, what if she didn't know the correct proportions of cement, sand and water to mix in order to pour a really solid foundation? Your beautifully planned home certainly wouldn't be built to bring you years of trouble-free enjoyment. Tracking activities are like those of the contractor. Their major function is to provide you with the crucial facts and figures you need to correctly build your "financial home" on a solid foundation.

The best architectural plans are of little value in the hands of an unskilled builder. Likewise, an excellent builder can do little without the details a good set of plans provides. In the same way, creating wonderful plans for wealth without tracking follow-up will result in a lot of really nice pie-in-the-sky fantasies—while world-class tracking skills without inspired creating will, at best, produce a good bookkeeper. When both actions are working in unison, your Financial Freedom is significantly easier to achieve.

As a psychological process, creating is done with the right side of the brain, which is responsible for intuition, spatial relations and abstract thinking. It thinks in broad concepts—the forest, not the trees.

The right side of your brain has to do with how you think about money-related events. What pictures do you hold in your mind's eye? Do you see yourself rich or poor? What do you tell yourself about how much you can have?

What, you might ask, does all this have to do with doubling your income or getting out of debt?

A lot.

As it turns out, a great deal of sports and business training these days has to do with learning how to actively visualize positive outcomes.

For example, if you were a member of the current U.S. Olympic downhill ski team, you'd spend a significant portion of every day closing your eyes and imagining yourself flawlessly skiing your downhill race in record time. Your coach would encourage you to use all your senses in your visualization. You'd be instructed to actually put yourself into the picture and experience the smell of the cold air, the colors of the flags as they go by, the sounds of the crowd, the emotional surge of competitive energy, the movements and flexibility of your body and, best of all, that wonderful feeling of success as you cross the finish line faster than everyone else—a gold medalist!

Why do they do this?

Because psychologists involved in brain research have discovered that the human mind doesn't clearly distinguish between actual behavior and a well-imagined fantasy. All you really need to know is this: You have a wonderful power in your mind that will help you become a success. All you have to do is learn to use it. And the Financial Freedom program is precisely designed to show you how to use it to become wealthy.

One key that researchers have found is that the more lifelike your fantasy, the stronger the possibility of your visualization becoming manifested in the real world. That's why championship skiers are encouraged to "smell" the air, "see" the colors of the flags, "hear" the sounds of the crowd and "feel" their bodies. These mental actions all add to the lifelike reality of their visualizations. (Our theory is that these actions also serve as supercharged input directions to their PALS.)

The main purpose of creating is to assist you in reeducating or reprogramming your mind for more positive outcomes. Notice we say "reeducating" and "reprogramming" rather than simply "educating" and "programming." This is because the present state of your finances is a direct result of the education or programming your mind has *already* received over the years.

Your current financial condition has previously been ingrained into your psychological makeup and will change only when new programming is both received and accepted by your PALS.

And new programming is precisely what Financial Freedom is all about.

Using your creating power effectively will do more to positively change your financial life than anything else we know. It will be a vital part of your program to increase your wealth—to be used in harmony with your tracking power.

Tracking behavior comes under the domain of the left side of your brain, which relies on reasoning that's rational, sequential and linear. It sees the trees, not the forest.

Examples of this type of activity include following step-by-step instructions, making lists and checking them off, doing mathematical calculations and storing specific bits of information. The left side of the brain thinks in straight lines. It goes from A to B to C, reducing things to the smallest possible steps. Your PALS are master trackers. They remember every instruction they have ever input in your current mental data banks—and they'll do everything they can to protect and maintain that information.

The tracking side of finances has to do with how you monitor your financial kingdom. Do you know what your accurate checkbook balance is? Are you aware of how much you spent on clothes last year? Have you planned exactly how you intend to generate a surplus of money next year? To not have the answers to questions such as these is like the contractor trying to build your home without the blueprint.

Simply put, tracking is *extremely* important. The more information you have, the better equipped your PALS are to effectively assist you in creating wealth. The more specific you can be in this area, the more effective you'll be at producing your intended result—Financial Freedom.

The types of things you'll need to do in order to become a better tracker are laid out for you in Part II of this book—simply and clearly. Most of the required actions are things you're probably already doing if you keep any financial records at all. They are activities such as accurately maintaining your checkbook, keeping track of income and expenses and organizing yourself in a way that makes it easier for you to do these things.

If you don't currently keep any financial records, don't worry. You can learn. All it takes is willingness and persistence. Since it's precisely the tracking aspect of money that many people find the most challenging, we've created easy-to-use forms with detailed step-by-step instructions to assist you. Implementing this tracking system will send a loud and clear message to your PALS: "I intend to become wealthy!"

Our basic point is this—you must learn to use your creative ability to visualize and hold a picture in your mind of your being wealthy. Then use your tracking skills to reinforce your commitment to financial success. The combined action of both creating and tracking working in harmony is what actually produces results. And it's the commitment and discipline of both *believing* new positive thoughts and *doing* new constructive behaviors that convinces your PALS that you mean to change.

Most people have a clear preference for either creating or tracking. Very few people enjoy and excel at both.

Your preference will have a direct effect on how you handle your finances. Those predominantly right-brained, creative people will be able to visualize well but may find implementing the tracking activities more challenging. Predominantly left-brained people often find the reverse to be true.

Because both creating and tracking are necessary to support sustained success, the Financial Freedom program focuses on how to effectively engage both sides of your brain. If you favor one of these types of actions, we'll encourage you to practice developing the other. This not only creates more financial success, it helps you practice using the power of your mind to your benefit— in ways that didn't necessarily come naturally before. The possibilities are endless, not the least of which include improvements in the areas of business, physical health and interpersonal relationships. (Believe it or not, another approach to consider is that if you're a tracker, marry a creator, and vice versa. That's what we did.)

GETTING THE BIG PICTURE

Here are the main points to keep in mind as you move ahead with your Financial Freedom program.

1. Within the realm of your mind, the thinking and behavioral habits you have are maintained by your PALS, whose job is to assist you in surviving by letting you know what has worked to keep you alive and functioning up until now. Your PALS will maintain the status quo to protect you. And you direct your PALS with your thoughts, your beliefs and your behavior.

2. The two functional systems of your mind that produce results are creating and tracking. The creating system is your architect, and the tracking system is your contractor. When both are working in harmony, fantastic results often appear.

3. Your finances, and the psychological systems that control them, are best changed by working at all levels of consciousness,

using an integrated and systematic approach. The essentials of this approach are:

- Transforming personal myths (mental level).
- Implementing new positive behaviors (physical level).
- Acknowledging feelings and nurturing positive emotions (emotional level).

At this point, you've already begun to transform some of your limiting personal myths about money. Now we begin the process of setting up your tracking system.

Part II

*"I am not fond of money, or anxious about it.
But, though every day makes me less and less eager
for wealth, every day shows me more and more
strongly how necessary a competence is to a man
who desires to be either great or useful."*

—THOMAS B. MACAULAY

YOUR PERSONAL
MONEY MANAGEMENT SYSTEM

WHY GO TO ALL
THE TROUBLE?

If getting wealthy is important to you, you must establish habits that clearly demonstrate your intention to wisely manage your money and build wealth.

How do you do that?

First, you learn to take care of the money you have. That includes caring for *yourself* in relationship to your money. You accomplish this by nurturing healthy thoughts and feelings about your finances.

Second, you demonstrate that you're prepared to handle the responsibility of even more money when it comes to you. That means cultivating attitudes and habits that show that you're ready, willing and able to become wealthy. One of the best ways to show this is to develop a well-organized, efficient money management system. This sends a clear message to your Private Access Learning System (PALS) that money is important to you and that you know how to care for it.

Your rewards for developing these money management habits? Well, one is that more money will be attracted to you. How's that for starters?

We've developed 11 steps to assist you in setting up an effective and efficient money management program. We call it Your Personal Money Management System—because it's designed by *you* to support you in reaching your goal of being wealthy. Our role will be to show you *exactly* how to use the system, step-by-step.

Our years of experience have shown us that for most people, this system actually takes *less time* than the one they currently use. And it drastically reduces the worry and emotional stress of managing money. (If you're anything like us, the less emotional stress, the better!)

So let's get started on Your Personal Money Management System. We'll help you create peace of mind as well as a clear map of your road to Financial Freedom.

What a deal!

CHAPTER
7

STEP 1: SETTING UP
YOUR FINANCIAL
ENVIRONMENT

Every successful company needs a corporate headquarters. This is the financial nerve center where all records are kept, cash flow is monitored, bills are paid and financial plans are made.

And that includes *your* million-dollar company, too!

The physical environment you create for managing your money is a very important step—so important that it can actually determine your success or failure at achieving an attitude of wealth.

Why?

Our years of financial counseling have shown us over and over that the environment you create to handle your finances makes a direct statement about your own feelings of self-worth.

Whether your self-worth is sky-high or in the pits, you've got a solid shot at financial success if you follow this simple instruction: Establish your corporate headquarters in a neat and organized setting.

75

Our experience shows that you'll get much better results if the financial habits you develop are associated with pleasant surroundings.

In other words, don't jam bills and bank statements into your night-table drawer along with tissues, paperbacks and cough drops. Stop balancing your checkbook while you're slurping down your morning coffee. No more paying your bills with one eye on the television.

Even if you don't believe it yet, act as if you *deserve* an uplifting environment in which to implement Your Personal Money Management System. We've found that consistently giving yourself a positive message through a well-organized and uplifting environment helps anchor the experience of worthiness inside you.

Why is this so important?

Because self-worth is a critical aspect of cultivating a consciousness of wealth.

CREATING YOUR FINANCIAL HEADQUARTERS

In setting up a financial nerve center in your home, the main issue is *not* size.

All that really counts is availability.

Sure, it would be great to have your own financial center complete with desktop computer. But it's far from a critical component. As a matter of fact, a small desk in your den or spare bedroom is just terrific. Even a kitchen or dining room table is a good place to get started, as long as it's *all yours* whenever you want to work with your finances.

MANAGEMENT TIP

How big a work area you have is less important than its availability for your regular money management sessions.

LAYING IN YOUR FINANCIAL SUPPLIES

After you've determined where in your home you're going to set up your corporate headquarters, the next step is to amass the tools you'll need to do your work. To really prepare yourself for success at managing your money, we recommend that you stock your headquarters with the following supplies. (All of them can be purchased inexpensively at most office supply stores or stationery stores. You even may already have most of them.)

Here's your shopping list for success.

- 12 file folders (These now come in an assortment of colors and sizes. No need to get legal size; regular size is fine.)
- 4 large envelopes (A good size is 9 × 12 inches.)
- 1 small desk calculator with memory function (Be sure it's capable of printing a tape showing all calculations.)
- 1 fine-tipped black pen (We use black because it works well in copy machines. Blue ink doesn't copy well on many older copiers.)
- 2 pencils (For copying purposes, we suggest #3 lead as a compromise between a fine point and a dark line.)
- 1 bar eraser or soap eraser (The erasers on the ends of most pencils dry out long before the pencils are used up.)
- 1 plastic or metal 6-inch ruler
- 1 stapler and box of staples
- 1 package medium-size rubber bands

SETTING YOUR OFFICE HOURS

Among the first questions our clients ask are "How much time do I have to spend on money management?" and "When is the best time to do my financial work?"

Our answer has always been the same: Like most successful businesses, it's best to have regular office hours.

A guideline that works for many people is: Small amounts of time on a regular basis save you large amounts of time later on.

Many of our clients tell us that doing their bill paying and record keeping *one evening every two weeks* is sufficient. (Since Your Personal Money Management System will be designed by

MANAGEMENT TIP ▮▿▿▿▿▿▿▿▿▿▿▿▿▿▿▿▿▿▿▿▿▿▿▿▿▮

 The more efficient you are in working with Your Personal Money Management System, the less time you'll actually need to spend doing it. That means you'll have more time for the things you love to do! Use this idea as an incentive to really fine-tune your system and get your work finished. That way, you'll have more time for what you really enjoy.

▮▲▲▲▲▲▲▲▲▲▲▲▲▲▲▲▲▲▲▲▲▲▲▲▲▲▲▲▲▲▲▲▲▮

you, you'll be able to tailor it so that it fits your needs and circumstances.)

One timesaving element we've learned is: Easy access to the tools and records you need is an important aspect of efficient money management.

So if your base of operation is a desk, then all your financial items, papers and records should be kept there. If you're using your kitchen or dining room table, then you'll want to store your financial records and supplies in something like a banker's box (a cardboard box with a lid). That way, all your records and tools are at your fingertips!

Be sure you put away all your records and supplies as soon as you finish your management session. Do not leave your papers, pens and file folders lying around. Why? It's important that you send clear, direct messages to your Private Access Learning System (PALS), such as "I'm dedicated to doing what it takes to create more wealth."

Things such as a sloppy work space or an incomplete work session send mixed messages to your PALS. In effect, you are saying to yourself "I may *say* that I'll do what it takes to attract more money, but I don't even think my financial work is important enough to straighten up or finish what I've started."

Mixed messages about your commitment to financial success make it very difficult to harness the positive, creative powers of your mind. Instead of helping you, your PALS decide "This person doesn't really want wealth, so let's just maintain the status quo and not support her in getting it."

YOUR FINANCIAL IN-BOX

Remember our client Elizabeth, the attorney who couldn't find her checkbook, bills or bank statements? She's only one of many clients we've consulted with who had challenges paying their bills and balancing their checkbooks because they couldn't find their bills or bank statements. Chances are good that you know someone who fits this description—maybe it's you!

One thing all these clients had in common was that they were *unconscious about their money.* In other words, like Elizabeth and her fear of debt, each of them did not want to face the state of his finances for some psychological reason. So they "went unconscious," as we say in the counseling trade.

Being conscious about your finances is an absolute necessity for successful money management. We go so far as to say that if you don't get conscious about your money, you'll never succeed at getting wealthy.

One of the first ways we assist our clients in breaking the habit of unconsciousness is to insist that they begin to use a *financial in-box.* We strongly suggest you do the same.

What does this mean?

Simply select a location in your home and consistently route all financial mail there *on the day it arrives.* This includes bills, bank statements, correspondence, checks received, investment dividends, credit card slips and similar items.

MANAGEMENT TIP ▮▾▾▾▾▾▾▾▾▾▾▾▾▾▾▾▾▾▾▾▾▾▾▮

 If you are using a desk as your financial center, try putting aside a special place in a desk drawer as your in-box. For those of you tight on space, a basket in the kitchen can work just as well.

Taking responsibility for your financial mail is an important part of the overall reprogramming of your PALS toward money and wealth. A financial in-box demonstrates that you're taking charge of your money. It's a way of communicating to yourself: "I value myself! I value my time and energy. I work smarter, not harder, thereby taking care of myself and my money."

▾▾▾▾▾▾▾▾▾▾▾▾▾▾▾▾▾▾▾▾▾▾▾▾▾▾▾▾▾▾▾▮

TIME LINES FOR YOUR FINANCIAL RECORDS

To help you set up an efficient corporate headquarters, here's important information on which financial records you should keep and how long to keep them. These guidelines are recommended by a leading tax preparation company.

Canceled checks. Seven years is the generally accepted guideline.

Income tax returns. If your tax return involves the sale of investment property, rental property or depreciation schedules, you should keep these records for at least five years after the sale of the property is completed. We strongly advise keeping your tax returns indefinitely. Believe it or not, the Internal Revenue Service (IRS) does make mistakes. For example, their records may show you didn't file a return when you really did.

(Speaking of tax returns—you may never have thought of this before—they can be like old photograph albums. Reviewing them years later can be a great way to appreciate where you've come from, what you've built, significant events and how your wealth has grown.)

Correspondence with the IRS. You may need proof of filing. It's best to always send your tax returns, as well as any other correspondence with the IRS, by certified mail with return receipts requested. Like your tax returns, keep all correspondence with the IRS indefinitely. (We keep any correspondence in a file folder accompanying our tax returns for the year the correspondence refers to.)

Real estate records. It's important to keep escrow papers, loan papers and bills for improvements on property indefinitely, as they're needed to determine matters such as capital gains taxes. This is because the current basis of evaluation of your home comes from the original cost plus the cost of improvements.

Records and bills regarding home improvements. Keep these indefinitely. If you ever sell your home, you'll have the documentation to establish any savings on capital gains taxes.

Estate settlement papers. The time recommended to keep these is between five and ten years. The more complicated the settlement process, the longer you want to keep the papers. (Personally, we recommend keeping them indefinitely.)

Credit card bills. Keep these three years, unless they pertain to tax-deductible expenses.

MENTAL TIP ▚▼▼▼▼▼▼▼▼▼▼▼▼▼▼▼▼▼▼▼▼▼▼▼▼▼▼▼▼▼▼▚

 Remember, for maximum success, it's psychologically important to create a pleasurable environment with as much order as possible.

▲▼▼▼▼▼▼▼▼▼▼▼▼▼▼▼▼▼▼▼▼▼▼▼▼▼▼▼▼▼▼▼▼▼▚

Tax-deductible expenses. You should save receipts, credit card records and other proof of deductions for five years from the due date of your income tax return or the filing date, whichever is later.

SETTING THE STAGE

We believe there's great value in structuring personal money management sessions in a supportive way. If you approach financial work as a grind, a necessary evil or, heaven forbid, homework, your thoughts will be counterproductive to creating wealth.

Instead, treat yourself with care and consideration while you're doing this very important work.

Here's how we support ourselves in doing *our* Personal Money Management System.

First, we decided that designating one room in our home as our financial center would work best for us.

In our headquarters, we have a library table where we do our work. On it is a Lucite in-box where we keep all financial mail and related papers to be processed, including credit card slips, forms to be submitted for medical insurance reimbursement and so forth.

All our financial records are in a nearby filing cabinet. Everything we need to do our Personal Money Management System is at our fingertips!

Oh, yes, all our heuristics are here, too. (These are lots of fun. We'll tell you all about them in Part III.)

Before starting to work, we often make a cup of hot chocolate, turn on some quiet music and maybe burn some cedar incense we get in Santa Fe (one of our favorite places to visit when our vacation fund permits). Weather permitting, we open the patio door so that we can hear the birds or smell the flowers.

Sound inviting?

As you can see, we're all for "treating" ourselves. Our years of experience have shown us that care and consideration toward ourselves make it much easier for us to focus on our financial work and to enter into a pleasant, positive state of mind about money.

ACTION STEPS

Here's a summary of what to do next to set up your financial environment. *Now* would be a great time to take these steps. But if that's not convenient, definitely schedule an appointment with yourself to do them.

1. Select your corporate headquarters, the place where you'll regularly implement Your Personal Money Management System.

2. Decide where you will be storing your financial records and supplies. You may need to buy a file cabinet or banker's box.

3. Select the place where you'll be accumulating all financial papers for processing. You may want to buy an in-box or use an empty drawer.

4. Make an appointment with yourself for your next money management session, which is reading chapter 8, "Step 2: Getting a Handle on Your Current Assets." Write down this appointment and keep it!

CHAPTER
8

STEP 2: GETTING
A HANDLE ON
YOUR CURRENT ASSETS

Congratulations on organizing your corporate headquarters and stocking it with supplies. Many of our clients tell us that setting up their offices results in a wonderful sense of empowerment, energy and anticipation.

We found this to be true for us also.

And we believe this reaction points out a key element in the powerful, and so far untapped, role your Private Access Learning System (PALS) can play in helping you create wealth.

PALS AS FINANCIAL PARTNERS

As you begin to take actions—such as organizing your personal financial headquarters—your PALS evaluate this new behavior as a signal that you're sincere in your intention to make major changes in the state of your financial health. In client after client, we've witnessed that when people express their intentions to **83** create wealth by taking concrete, specific actions, their PALS support them. Yours will, too. And one of the great rewards is that *your PALS willingly free up more mental and physical energy* to support you in moving forward with Your Personal Money Management System.

This is why we constantly stress the importance of intention and willingness to build new, more positive habits. As your intention to build wealth and manifest Financial Freedom grows stronger, the methods you can use to make these things happen will become clearer to you. One thing is crystal clear to us: *Your incredibly powerful PALS are ready, willing and able to give you all the information, support and guidance you need to achieve your financial goals.*

GETTING THE BIG PICTURE

It's been said that if you want to know where you're going, begin by determining where you're starting from. We think this is great advice for anyone on the road to Financial Freedom.

To help you get this crucial information, we'll use one of the keys presented in chapter 1, "Meet the President of a Million-Dollar Company: You!"—*honest assessment*.

We refer to this part of Your Personal Money Management System as "viewing financial scenes" because you are going to literally create a view, in picture form, of your financial situation. In our years of fiscal counseling, we've determined that most people respond best if they can get an overview of their finances at a glance.

The very first financial scene you need to construct is Current Assets. In simple language, this will create a picture of everything you've got that's worth some money. Or think of it this way: How much would you have if you made a pile of everything you own and assigned an accurate value to it all?

Call us crazy, but we love the image of everybody counting and evaluating great big piles of their stuff. We laugh every time we think of it. (Probably because we're nuts about George Carlin's great comic monologue on the ridiculousness of the human animal's propensity to gather, guard and worship his "stuff.")

We hope you find humor in this concept, too, because laughter and lightheartedness are keys to success when you're dealing with finances . . . especially when you're faced with assigning a value to your assets. We've found that some people—maybe you're one of them—are so challenged by the very idea of evaluating their assets that they absolutely resist doing it.

In our experience with people who resist getting a good honest look at their financial situation, the hitch has always been this: *They have their self-worth confused with their financial worth.*

We live in a culture that holds to certain distorted values, such as "He who dies with the most toys wins." You can see how some of us get confused about our self-worth. This can be very painful, especially because most of us don't yet have the money or assets we feel we want, need or deserve. If you don't have a healthy attitude toward viewing your assets, you can set yourself up to feel like a failure. And that is *not* the purpose of this exercise.

That's where humor can really help. Assets have absolutely nothing to do with your worth as a human being. They're just things, items, doohickeys that have a monetary value. We really encourage you to remember the image of everybody counting great big piles of their stuff. And if you've never heard Carlin's hysterical stand-up routine about "stuff" (on his tape *A Place for My Stuff*), perhaps you'd benefit from listening to it before creating a financial scene of your assets. You especially need to listen to it if the idea evokes strong emotions, such as fear, anger, insecurity or the desire to shut this book and never open it again.

A Little Help from the Banks (Family)

What are your personal company's financial assets *right now?*

That's the question we want to answer in our next step toward greater financial health.

Don't worry. We won't actually ask you to count up all your towels, socks, spoons and so on, but we will ask you to evaluate certain specific items as we go along.

To help you create your own financial scenes, we've developed several special forms for you to complete. Since most people learn best from example, we've created a sample family so that you can see these forms used successfully.

We call them the Banks family. There's a husband named Rich, a wife named Goldie and two young children, Silver and Buck. Oops! We almost forgot their faithful dog, Wealthy.

All the samples in this book were done using this family's finances. We've made these assumptions about Rich, Goldie and the kids: They live in California and own a modest home. Rich works full-time at a salaried position, and he and Goldie share in running a small sideline mail-order business. They started to implement their Financial Freedom program in July 1993. They named their million-dollar firm the Rich and Goldie Banks Company.

If you turn to the sample form on page 88, you can immediately see that July 10, 1993, is the date Rich and Goldie took charge of this part of their Personal Money Management System. Next you'll notice the various arms and lines extending from the Financial Freedom heart. Each of these arms identifies one aspect of Rich and Goldie's financial situation. Together they are all part of this family's wealth and, in financial lingo, are called *assets*.

Before we ask you to determine *your* assets and create your own Current Assets scene, let's look at each of the Banks family's assets. This will really help you understand the process.

CURRENT ASSETS: THE RICH AND GOLDIE BANKS COMPANY

Let's go around the heart, right to left.

Certificate of deposit. This is a bank investment and is usually referred to as a CD. Its value as of July 10, 1993, was $27,100, and it can be cashed in at the time of maturity, which can vary from a matter of days to several years.

Home equity. The best way we know to find the current market value for your home is to have it appraised and then subtract the balance remaining on your mortgage. If you own your home free and clear, its appraised value is the amount of your equity.

One way to obtain a free appraisal of your home annually is to have a gentlemen's agreement with a real estate agent who'll tour your home and give you a realistic estimate of what it could sell for on the current market. Then at the beginning of each year, you call the agent, who can advise you of any changes in your home's value based on sales of comparable properties in your area. In return for this service, you agree that when and if you decide to sell, you'll call the agent first and allow her to be the listing agent. We've found most agents more than happy to have this kind of arrangement with you.

Home equity of the Banks family: $23,000.

Business. There are many variables to consider in establishing a value for a business. These include: how profitable it is, how important you are to its success, the inventory and equipment needed to maintain it, the time required to run it, how much expertise is necessary and to what degree you possess such expertise. In the case of the Banks family, the business is small, very lucrative, requires very little equipment and inventory and isn't heavily dependent upon the personalities of the people who run it. Rich and Goldie spend about six to eight hours a week on their business.

The value of $36,000 was established by taking into consideration that the business has a history of consistently generating $12,000 annual profits from $15,600 in sales over the past few years and has been growing slightly. If a buyer was to pay $36,000 for this business, he would be paying three times the annual earnings, which, given the assumptions outlined, is a conservative estimate. The buyer could reasonably expect to have made back his investment in three years. From then on, the business would throw off profits.

From a business perspective, this is an attractive proposition for someone looking for such a sideline. It's even more attractive to a buyer familiar with the mail-order business who sees specific ways to quickly increase sales.

Cash on hand. This is money Rich and Goldie keep around the house for unexpected needs. They had $380 in cash.

Automobiles. An easy way to determine the current value of your autos is to periodically buy one or two issues of auto trade magazines that specialize in used cars in your area. Using the year and model of your car, look for the ones most similarly equipped. You can easily come within a few hundred dollars of the cash value of your auto(s) this way.

The Banks family owns two cars, both of which are a few years old and together were valued at $11,700.

Life insurance cash value. Very often life insurance policies have a cash surrender value. This means that if you tell the insur-

THE BANKS FAMILY'S CURRENT ASSETS

As of July 10, 1993

Certificate of Deposit (CD)-$27,100

Home Equity-$23,000
(current appraised value
less outstanding mortgage)

Money Owed to You-$0

Retirement Funds-$12,400
(IRA, Keogh, annuities, etc.)

Business-$36,000
(conservative estimate of net worth)

Personal Property-$7,050
(art, jewelry, antiques,
gold coins, etc.)

Cash on Hand-$380

Marketable Securities-$9,000
(mutual funds, stocks, bonds, etc.)

Automobiles-$11,700
(conservative appraised value)

Checking Accounts-$6,076

Life Insurance Cash Value-$2,800

TOTAL ASSETS $135,506

ance company you want to end your coverage and cash in your policy, the insurer pays you a sum of money, dependent upon how long you've had the policy and how much coverage you have. Here the cash surrender value was $2,800.

Checking accounts. This amount is found by determining the current balance in your checking accounts.

Rich and Goldie's balance was $6,076.

Marketable securities. These are investments that can be sold simply by calling your investment broker and directing her to sell. One way to find a security's current value is to ask your broker the price it's trading for today. Another way is to check the section of the *Wall Street Journal* that lists the current value of your particular investments. The Banks family has some mutual funds and a few stocks, with a total value of $9,000 as of July 10, 1993.

Personal property. What we're really saying when we consider personal property is: "What is the market value of a particular item if I sell it today?"

Sometimes people find it challenging to think this way because a certain object has been inherited or was a gift from a loved one. While these items may have considerable sentimental value, unless they can be turned into significant cash, we feel it's best to value them at $0.

The Banks family owns wedding rings, a few lithographs, an inherited necklace and two gold coins given to Silver and Buck by their grandfather. The best way for you to find the actual financial value of these kinds of items is to call in a professional appraiser (if you think the property has considerable value). You could also visit a local vendor who deals in the type of items you have and ask him to tell you the market value if you were to sell them today.

If you think an appraisal is necessary, consult the Yellow Pages of your telephone directory under "Appraisers." We suggest you do comparison shopping by calling a few and telling them exactly what you want done.

An appraisal of the Banks family's personal property placed its marketable value at $7,050.

Retirement funds. These assets are somewhat unique. While they do have financial value, they're usually invested in an individual retirement account (IRA) or a pension fund. You probably wouldn't tap them because there's frequently a penalty (unless you're already at retirement age). Even though it may not be all that available to spend, the money involved is certainly part of your assets.

Rich and Goldie had $12,400 in retirement money.

Money owed to you. This category can sometimes be a challenge. For instance, maybe you've loaned money to a close friend or relative. While the person's intention was clear at the time, it may not be clear to you now whether or not you're ever going to be repaid. For purposes of your Current Assets scene, we suggest that if you sincerely question whether you'll ever see the money, it's best to assign no dollar value to the loan. Rich and Goldie had no money owed to them.

Total assets. The assets of the Rich and Goldie Banks Company, when totaled, equaled $135,506. That number appears in the box at the bottom of the form.

CREATING YOUR COMPANY'S FINANCIAL SCENE

Now it's time to take your next big step. As they used to say on "Mission Impossible": "It's your assignment, if you choose to accept it." (We hope you do.)

On page 217, you'll find some suggestions on the easiest way to use the forms. Then on page 220, you'll find a blank Current Assets form for your use.

Here are some pointers on successfully completing a Current Assets scene.

▪ Since the particulars of most peoples' finances vary, all the Banks family's categories may not be relevant to you. Don't worry. Simply use the ones that fit for you. And add any that are your very own, such as real estate or investment-quality art collections.

▪ Be as precise as you can when filling in the form, and at the same time, feel free to make educated guesses if the information isn't readily available. (It's important, however, to get the accurate information as soon as you can.)

▪ Write in pencil, as you may find more information you'll want to add later.

ACTION STEPS 〜〜〜〜〜〜〜〜〜〜〜〜〜〜〜〜

1. Make a list of your assets.

2. Financially evaluate each asset.

3. Enter your assets on the blank Current Assets form.

4. Get a file folder and label it "Assets, Debt, Net Worth, Cash Flow—1994" (or whatever year you're beginning) and place your Current Assets form in it.

5. Make an appointment with yourself for your next money management session, which is reading chapter 9, "Step 3: Facing Your Current Debt."

CHAPTER
9

STEP 3: FACING YOUR
CURRENT DEBT

*D*ebt. If the very sound of the word makes you feel like someone's turned up the heat in the room, believe us, you're not alone. In our 20 years of financial counseling, we've found that talking about debt can be one of the most emotionally loaded experiences people face.

Many people have their mental wires crossed about the concept of debt. Believe it or not, being in debt does *not* put you in a moral category right below Ivan Boesky or Lady Macbeth. Debt is simply another opportunity to *learn* how to be successful with your money.

For many of us, the word *debt* trips off an unconscious alarm that screams "Bad girl!" or "Bad boy!" in a voice that lets you know you've really done something wrong. (It's the same tone you use to frantically yell "Bad doggie!" at the pooch that's chewing up your brand-new Reeboks.)

MENTAL TIP ▐▼▼▼▼▼▼▼▼▼▼▼▼▼▼▼▼▼▼▼▼▼▼▼▼▼▼▼▼▼▼▼▼▌

The key to success with debt is all in your attitude. And the winning attitude toward creating a scene of your current debt is: No matter what the amount you owe (or how judgmental the voice in your head), being aware of your real debt picture is the first step in bringing it to zero.

▐▼▼▼▼▼▼▼▼▼▼▼▼▼▼▼▼▼▼▼▼▼▼▼▼▼▼▼▼▼▼▼▼▼▌

CURRENT DEBT ASSESSMENT:
THE RICH AND GOLDIE BANKS COMPANY

Before you fill out your Current Debt Assessment form on page 221, let's check in with the Banks family (remember our sample family?) and view *its* financial scene.

The Banks Family's Current Debt Assessment form on page 94 presents a straightforward view of Rich and Goldie's debt. It's simply a list of all they owed, including to whom they owed, the outstanding balances, the rates of interest, the minimum monthly payments and the number of payments remaining.

In reviewing the Banks family's debt picture, you'll notice that all debts aren't set up the same way. For example, auto loans usually involve regular monthly payments of a set amount scheduled to be paid over a clearly defined number of months. Credit card debts, on the other hand, usually have a minimum monthly payment required but no set number of payments remaining.

The Banks family's list of debts includes all money Rich and Goldie owed—with the exception of the family's home mortgage balance. Why?

Homes are psychologically perceived as *investments* that appreciate in value over time. We don't experience our home as a consumer item that is used up over time. That's why we dealt with the mortgage on the Banks Family's Current Assets form in step 2. For purposes of getting an accurate view of a family's finances, we take the current home equity (current appraised value less outstanding mortgage) and treat it as an *asset.*

Let's take a look at each of the Banks family's debts as they appear on the form.

THE BANKS FAMILY'S
CURRENT DEBT ASSESSMENT

July 10, 1993

Owed to	Amount Owed	Annual Interest Rate	Minimum Monthly Payments	Payments Remaining
Visa	$ 797	15.3%	$ 24	0
MasterCard	$ 464	15.3%	$ 15	0
My parents	$ 500	0	$ 50	10
Robinson's Department Store	$ 370	19.8%	$ 50	0
Auto loans	$ 5,600	9.5%	$ 140	48
Totals	**$ 7,731**		**$ 279**	

■ The first two are credit card debts and, as such, had no specific number of payments remaining.

■ The next entry is an interest-free loan from Goldie's parents. It was scheduled to be repaid at the rate of $50 per month over a ten-month period.

■ The department store bill works the same as a credit card issued by a bank. There's a minimum monthly payment (in this case, $50) but no set number of payments remaining. Notice the interest on any unpaid balance is a hefty 19.8 percent.

■ Last, their auto loans still had $5,600 owed at 9.5 percent annual interest, which meant a minimum monthly payment of $140. Rich and Goldie had fours years remaining on their auto loans.

Total debt picture: When all the family's debts were totaled, they equaled $7,731. That required Rich and Goldie to make total monthly payments of $279 to service these debts.

YOUR FIRST STEP TO A DEBT-FREE LIFE

In these difficult times—when so many people have a considerable amount of debt—taking an accurate look at exactly how much you owe can be truly challenging. That's why lots of people choose to avoid viewing an accurate scene of their current debt. Instead, they stumble along, hoping that things will somehow work themselves out. You can bet your assets that these people will never experience true financial health!

So take a deep breath, relax, and turn your attention to the blank Current Debt Assessment form on page 221.

For our present purposes of viewing your financial scenes, all you need to do right now is determine your total debt by simply making a list of the outstanding balance owed to each of your creditors and then adding up the balances. In other words, complete the parts of the form labeled "Owed to" and "Amount Owed." When you've added up the list under "Amount Owed," you've successfully computed your current debt. This is really all the information you need to move on to step 4. However, we strongly encourage you to gather the rest of the information necessary to complete the form (annual interest rates, minimum monthly payments and payments remaining) when time permits. Only with a fully completed form will you have your entire debt picture at a glance.

For those of you willing to create a picture of your current debt, we salute you. And we strongly suggest that you take a break *right now* to praise yourself for your willingness to honestly look at what you owe. You've got a great attitude!

Feel the positive energy? Now get going!

MENTAL TIP ▚▼▼▼▼▼▼▼▼▼▼▼▼▼▼▼▼▼▼▼▼▼▼▼▼▼▼▼▚

The Financial Freedom heart appears on the Current Debt Assessment form, just as it does on many other forms, to remind you that all aspects of money, including debt, can be viewed with an attitude of abundance, prosperity and heartfelt caring.

▼▼▼▼▼▼▼▼▼▼▼▼▼▼▼▼▼▼▼▼▼▼▼▼▼▼▼▼▼▼▼▼▼▼▼

ACTION STEPS

1. Gather the information about everyone you owe money to and how much you owe.

2. Use this information to complete the following categories on your Current Debt Assessment form: "Owed to," "Amount Owed" and "Totals."

3. Place your Current Debt Assessment form in the "Assets, Debt, Net Worth, Cash Flow" file folder.

4. Make an appointment with yourself to read chapter 10, "Step 4: Viewing Your Net Worth," and keep the appointment.

5. Make an appointment with yourself to complete the rest of the information on the Current Debt Assessment form and keep the appointment.

CHAPTER *10*

STEP 4: VIEWING
YOUR NET WORTH

Remember your great big pile of stuff from step 2? You figured out your assets, gulped hard and valiantly assigned them a cash value. All the while trying to convince yourself—perhaps unsuccessfully— "My financial worth is *not* my self-worth." We've often thought it interesting that "net worth" applies to how much we have financially while "self-worth" refers to how much we have psychologically.

Then in step 3, you turned up the heat and faced the total balance due on all your debts. That's a brave act yet to be done by a majority of your fellow humans.

Well, now comes the Mother of All Financial Computations. We're going to figure out your *net worth*. (Yikes, do we hear teeth rattling?)

What is your net worth?

About five bucks. (Sorry, we couldn't help injecting Groucho Marx into the midst of these ominous proceedings.)

In financial lingo, *net worth* is the "excess of assets over liabilities." (Huh?) Or "the residual equity of an owner after all debts have been paid." (Come again?)

To us, the clearest, easiest and least emotional way to think of net worth is this: You start with the cash value of your great big pile of stuff. Then you take away from the pile the amount of your debts. What's left over is your net worth. (Voilà!)

NET WORTH: THE RICH AND GOLDIE BANKS COMPANY

For an example of how to compute your net worth, let's return to the financial domain of our example, the Banks family. Below you'll find The Banks Family's Net Worth form, complete with all the figures for the Banks family.

The first entry is "Total Assets." The amount of $135,506 was derived from the information on the Banks Family's Current Assets form on page 88.

The second entry is "Total Debts." The amount of $7,731 reflects the information gathered on the Banks Family's Current Debt Assessment form on page 94. The next entry is "Net Worth." The amount of $127,775 was arrived at by subtracting the Banks family's debts (line 2 on that form) from its assets (line 1).

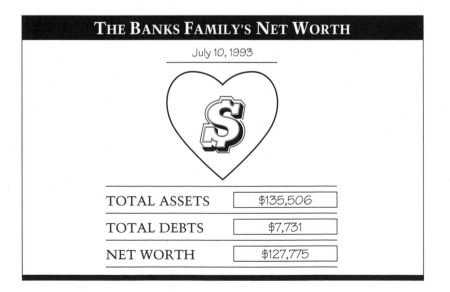

THE BANKS FAMILY'S NET WORTH

July 10, 1993

TOTAL ASSETS	$135,506
TOTAL DEBTS	$7,731
NET WORTH	$127,775

LET'S DO IT!

Okay, all you captains of your own million-dollar companies. Prepare to accurately figure out the most important dollar amount you've calculated in years.

Why?

Because net worth is the Official Starting Point from which you will launch not only Your Personal Money Management System but also your program for becoming wealthy.

To arrive at this all-important piece of personal financial information, you're going to fill in the blank Net Worth form on page 222. To do this, you'll need to refer to the two forms you've already filled out. (This may sound a little complicated, but if you take it one step at a time, it's a cinch.) First look at your Current Assets form. Find the figure at the bottom in the "Total Assets" box. Enter that figure on your blank Net Worth form. Now look at the Current Debt Assessment form that you already filled out. Take the total "Amount Owed" figure from the bottom and transfer that to your Net Worth form.

Now simply subtract your total debts from your total assets. Place the figure in the "Net Worth" box and pat yourself on the back.

NEGATIVE NUMBERS AND TOTAL HONESTY

We've counseled enough people to know that after looking at your bottom line, you are probably not about to dance all night. In fact, you may more likely want to pull the covers over your head.

If you feel like hiding in the dark, you probably fall into one of two categories.

You just found out that your current assets are greater than your current debts. And while this means your net worth is a positive number, it sure isn't *positive enough* for you. You were sure your assets were worth more money than that!

You just found out that your current debts are greater than your current assets. If this is the case, your net worth is a negative number. You may want to forgo the covers and immediately hide under the bed.

Important news flash for the anxious, worried and/or nauseated: Right now, it is not—we repeat, *not*—important whether your net worth is positive or negative.

To successfully begin Your Personal Money Management System, *all you need to do is accurately establish where you are starting from.* What's important right now is not the amount of money (positive *or* negative) but the *accuracy* of the figure.

Don't think you're getting away with anything by fudging these figures. They're for your benefit, not to impress your friends and relatives. You will only hurt your chances of achieving wealth by lying to yourself.

We say this because our 20 years of financial counseling have shown us that human consciousness, like Mother Nature, can't be fooled.

YOU HAVE A CHOICE!

Right now, you're at a critical point in establishing a personal money management program that can be a firm foundation for your financial success. This may well be the first time you've ever had an accurate view of your assets, debts and net worth. And likewise, you may not especially like what you see. In short, you want more money.

If you're going to be a winner at mastering money, now is the time to take to heart the advice that *who you are* has nothing to do with how much or how little money you have at any given time in your life.

You have a choice about viewing your current financial scenes. You can choose to bemoan your fate and judge yourself as a failure. *Or you can seize the opportunity to change your financial picture.*

If you see yourself as a failure, you're doing negative thinking. You are actually hurting yourself both psychologically and financially. Stop right now, turn back to chapter 5, "Transforming Your Personal Money Myths," and reread about negative thinking, negative beliefs and the consciousness of wealth.

If you're destined for financial success, you'll see your current financial state as an exciting challenge—in fact, a golden opportunity. You'll tell yourself that you're about to learn a dynamic new method for dealing with money that will powerfully alter your financial picture to include abundance, prosperity and success.

The choice is yours. We strongly suggest that you opt for opportunity!

ACTION STEPS ~~~~~~~~~~~~~~~~~~~~~~~~~~~~~~~~

1. If you've not already done so, complete the blank Net Worth form on page 222.

2. Place your completed Net Worth form in the "Assets, Debt, Net Worth, Cash Flow" file folder.

3. Make an appointment with yourself to read chapter 11, "Step 5: Getting a Look at Current Cash Flow," and keep that appointment.

4. Go see a fun movie!

CHAPTER *11*

STEP 5: GETTING
A LOOK AT
CURRENT CASH FLOW

Now that you've completed the momentous task of calculating your current assets, debts and net worth, we've got some surprising—and seemingly contradictory—news for you.

Critical as this information is to your financial health, on a *day-to-day* basis these are *not* the most important figures you'll deal with to achieve successful money management.

The two financial categories that you'll work with most intimately and regularly are:

- Income.
- Expenses.

Simply put: *Income is what comes to you each month, and expenses are what goes out.*

THE ESSENCE OF FINANCIAL HEALTH

The relationship between income and expenses determines whether your million-dollar company is oper-

ating in what the financial world calls positive or negative cash flow.

Positive cash flow means that you have more money coming in every month than is going out. *Negative cash flow* means that you have more money going out every month than is coming in.

Living in positive cash flow is the essence of Financial Freedom. If you truly have more coming in each month than is going out, all the surplus can be added to your *assets*. Doing this, along with wise investing, is what makes your assets grow over time. Positive cash flow is an essential part of the process of building wealth.

CURRENT CASH FLOW: THE RICH AND GOLDIE BANKS COMPANY

Let's return to the continuing saga of the Banks family's fortune by turning our attention to Rich and Goldie's Current Cash Flow form on page 104.

Please notice that directly beneath the words "Banks Family's Current Cash Flow," Rich and Goldie entered the notation "Estimated—1993." This lets us know that Rich and Goldie are measuring cash flow on an annual basis. This form then represents their projected income and expenses for 1993, the year the Banks family embarked on its conscious journey toward Financial Freedom.

You can see that the Banks family's form is divided into two halves: the left side for "Estimated Income," and the right for "Estimated Expenses."

Important note: Remember that all the entries on this form are

MANAGEMENT TIP ▾▾▾▾▾▾▾▾▾▾▾▾▾▾▾▾▾▾▾▾▾

We strongly suggest that you consider your cash flow annually. The reason is income tax. Most people pay income tax yearly, and as you'll soon see, taxes are a significant variable in figuring cash flow.

▴▴▴▴▴▴▴▴▴▴▴▴▴▴▴▴▴▴▴▴▴▴▴▴▴

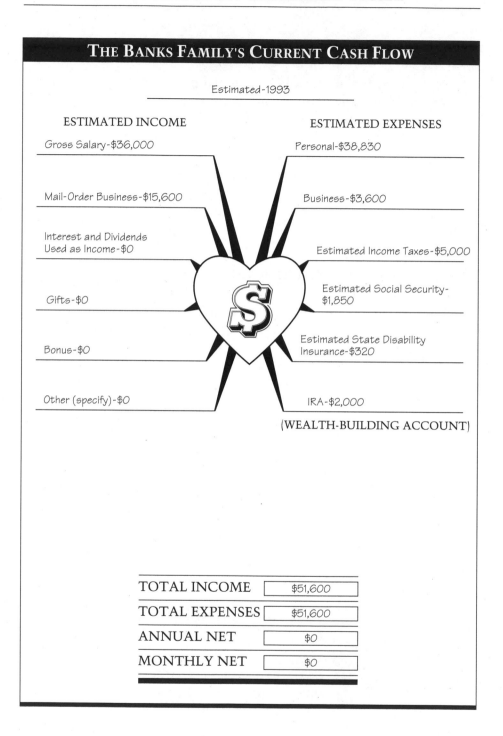

THE BANKS FAMILY'S CURRENT CASH FLOW

Estimated-1993

ESTIMATED INCOME

Gross Salary-$36,000

Mail-Order Business-$15,600

Interest and Dividends
Used as Income-$0

Gifts-$0

Bonus-$0

Other (specify)-$0

ESTIMATED EXPENSES

Personal-$38,830

Business-$3,600

Estimated Income Taxes-$5,000

Estimated Social Security-
$1,850

Estimated State Disability
Insurance-$320

IRA-$2,000

(WEALTH-BUILDING ACCOUNT)

TOTAL INCOME	$51,600
TOTAL EXPENSES	$51,600
ANNUAL NET	$0
MONTHLY NET	$0

MANAGEMENT TIP ▗▚▚▚▚▚▚▚▚▚▚▚▚▚▚▚▚▚▚▚▚▚▚▚

It's very difficult to know what your taxes are really going to be prior to the end of the year. However, you can get a fairly accurate estimate from your tax preparer.

▚▚▚▚▚▚▚▚▚▚▚▚▚▚▚▚▚▚▚▚▚▚▚▚▚▚▚▚▚▚▚

"best guesstimates." They represent what Rich and Goldie *thought* would happen with respect to their income and expenses. The same will be true for you. You'll be "guesstimating" your income and expenses on your form.

Let's look at Rich and Goldie's "Estimated Income."

■ What we see entered first is Rich's gross salary from his job. (That's his salary before taxes and other deductions were made.)

■ Then we see the additional money the family earned from its mail-order business.

■ Next we see an entry called "Interest and Dividends Used as Income," which shows $0. This simply means that any income earned from bank interest or dividends was either earned in or transferred to their Wealth-Building Account and *was not used to pay bills.* (We'll explain this in greater detail in step 6.)

■ The Banks family received no monetary gifts, bonuses or other income.

■ If we total their two sources of income, the estimated amount is $51,600. This figure was entered at the bottom of the form in the box for "Total Income."

Now let's check on the Banks family's "Estimated Expenses."

■ "Personal" refers to everything the family spent, *except for the money Rich and Goldie spent on their business.*

■ "Business" lists all money spent to run the mail-order business.

■ Next are estimated income taxes.

■ On the other hand, you can fill out the next entries—"Estimated Social Security" and "Estimated State Disability Insurance"—from your pay stubs.

■ You'll see that the entry for the individual retirement account (IRA) is at the very bottom of the "Estimated Expenses" column.

Here's why.

For purposes of accounting, the $2,000 is really an expense. In other words, it was "paid out," just like any other bill. However, the money was actually *paid to* Rich and Goldie by placing it into their IRA.

■ When added, Rich and Goldie's "best guess" regarding their expenses for the year was $51,600. This figure was entered in the bottom box for "Total Expenses."

THE CASE OF THE NOTABLE NET

As we continue to turn financial lingo into plain ol' English, here's the next fiscal mystery we must crack in order to progress: What in the world is an *annual net*—and why should you bother to find out?

Annual net is simply the difference between total income and total expenses. To compute your annual net, you subtract your total expenses from your total income. (In the case of the Banks family, we see that Rich and Goldie were projecting an annual net surplus for the year of $0.)

Far more interesting, however, is the answer to *why* you should discover your annual net.

You see, computing your annual net is the only way for you to answer this very critical question: "Assuming the accuracy of my estimated income and expenses, will I—or will I not—increase my wealth this year and by how much?"

While Rich and Goldie projected a net surplus of $0, they did, in fact, save $2,000, which was wisely placed in their Wealth-Building Account. They selected to invest these funds in their IRA.

Just how will Rich and Goldie Banks have fared? They will have increased their wealth by $2,000, which represents 3.88 per-

MANAGEMENT TIP ▚▚▚▚▚▚▚▚▚▚▚▚▚▚▚▚▚▚

The earlier in the year you fund your IRA, the more interest you'll earn, since you'll be earning it over a longer period of time.

cent of their total gross income. As you can see, this is far less than the minimum of 10 percent that we recommend to achieve true financial health.

If Rich and Goldie had put away 10 percent, they would have increased their wealth by $5,160—of which $2,000 might have gone into an IRA, leaving another $3,160 to invest toward financial independence!

FIGURING EXPENSES

Now it's *your* turn as President of a million-dollar company to take on the task of computing your company's cash flow. Turn to page 223, and you'll find a blank Current Cash Flow form on which you can calculate your estimated income and expenses and then determine the relationship between them—*your annual net.*

If you start Your Personal Money Management System early in the calendar year, your numbers will be based mostly on last year's figures. They'll be "projections" of what you expect this year. If you're starting later in the year, your numbers will be based primarily on what has already happened in that current year.

For most of us, income is easier to figure than expenses because we receive an income statement attached to each paycheck. Or we can determine our income from checkbook deposits or last year's income tax return.

Accurately figuring your past expenses is more challenging, especially if you haven't been keeping records. (Sound familiar?)

Based on our years of financial work with clients, we know that right now is one of the moments in money management counseling when many people choose to quit, run, hide or slam the book shut.

Why?

This part feels too hard, too frightening—or just plain impossible. Believe us, we understand that you may well be hard-pressed to write down an accurate assessment of your expenses—and that, in fact, you might not even have a clue as to what they really are.

There's nothing *wrong* with that. So please don't judge yourself as stupid, a failure, a bad money manager or whatever negative beliefs you may be beating yourself up with.

None of them is the reason you "can't" rattle off your expenses.

The simple reason is this: At this time, you don't have the information necessary for the task.

EMERGENCY AID
FOR THE EXPENSE-IMPAIRED

We can even show you how to *get* the information you need to estimate your expenses. No problem!

The most thorough method is to sit down and literally go through a year's worth of check stubs, checkbook log entries or canceled checks. Add them up, one month's worth at a time. (We'll assume that by now you've purchased your printing calculator.) This way, any unusually large monthly balances can alert you to *one-time-only* expenditures (such as a brand-new, state-of-the-art sound system).

A shorter way is to add up three months' worth of checks and multiply that figure by 4. This is good for people who haven't been consistently logging expenses in their checkbook . . . or who don't have an entire year's worth of canceled checks. (Remember Elizabeth, the attorney who couldn't find all her bank statements?) Since most expenses tend to be repetitive, this method generates a fairly accurate estimate. *However, you need to be careful that*

MENTAL TIP ▰▲▼▲▼▲▼▲▼▲▼▲▼▲▼▲▼▲▼▲▼▲▼▲▼▲▼▲▰

During the time you're figuring your income and expenses, you should describe your situation with statements that therapists refer to as "neutral." That means you're not using emotionally loaded words to describe what you're feeling. You don't, for example, say "See, I've always been lousy with money" or "How can I be so dumb as to not know how much I've spent?" Instead, you objectively and accurately present the facts, not your feelings. As you proceed to launch Your Personal Money Management System, strive to use "neutral" statements in describing the tasks at hand. Removing the emotional "ickiness" from your relationship with money will go a long way toward establishing a positive attitude of wealth.

▲▼▲▼▲▼▲▼▲▼▲▼▲▼▲▼▲▼▲▼▲▼▲▼▲▼▲▼▲▼▲▼▲▼▲▼▲▼▲

large expenses, such as insurance and tax payments, are taken into account.

If you have been using your checkbook consistently, here's a quick method: Look at your checkbook balance as of December 31 *for the most recent year for which you have complete figures.* Write down that figure.

Then look at the balance as of December 31 of the year before that and write down that number.

Then add up all your income for last year and use the formula shown in the following example.

> Your December 31, 1992, checkbook balance
> + Your 1993 income (assuming it was all deposited in
>   your checking account)
> − Your December 31, 1993, checkbook balance
> = Your 1993 expenses

Of course, if you haven't been using your checkbook very much, this method won't work for you.

COMPUTING YOUR CASH FLOW

Before you start filling out your form, read these attitude boosters.

Don't fret. Remember that most of the information on this form is likely to be based on estimates. Don't get hung up trying to get it exactly on the penny. Just take your best guess.

Do it now. Don't wait until January 1, April 15 or your birthday to get started. It doesn't matter in what month you begin. What matters is that you begin as soon as possible!

Use a pencil. This lets you know that you don't have to be exact or perfect. A pencil gives you permission to change the figures later on, when you have more accurate information about your income and expenses.

Give yourself a break. Aim for emotional neutrality. What if you should discover that your projected expenses are more than your income? Will you automatically give in to self-judgment and negative thinking? (*"I'm a complete failure!"*) If you do, *stop it!* Instead, honestly enter the information on the form. Stick to just the facts, not the feelings. The facts: You have just established a starting point in Your Personal Money Management System, no

MANAGEMENT TIP ▛▼▼▼▼▼▼▼▼▼▼▼▼▼▼▼▼▼▼▼▼▼▼▼▼▼▌

 If you don't have a checking account, we suggest that you open one. As we go forward in developing Your Personal Money Management System, you'll find that your checkbook will become an indispensable tool, making your financial life much easier. Why? Your canceled checks will serve as a receipt, showing you how much you've paid, to whom and for what.

▙▲▲▲▲▲▲▲▲▲▲▲▲▲▲▲▲▲▲▲▲▲▲▲▲▲▲▲▲▲▲▲▲▲▲▲▲▲▲▟

matter what the amount. To help reinforce this neutral view, try thinking of a runner beginning a race. Accept your annual net the way a runner accepts the starting line: It's just the place from which the race begins.

Enjoy your accomplishment. This is a one-time-only task. Once you've completed your Current Assets and Current Cash Flow forms, you'll never need to do them again! As you'll be glad to discover, Your Personal Money Management System is designed so that once you've gathered this financial information, your program automatically generates the next year's figures. Whew!

ACTION STEPS

1. Complete the "Estimated Income" side of the Current Cash Flow form using either accurate figures or honest best guesses—whichever are available for the current year.

2. Complete the "Estimated Expenses" side, including estimates of income taxes, Social Security, state disability insurance and so on.

3. Calculate your estimated annual net and average monthly net.

4. Estimate how much you will place in your Wealth-Building Account this year.

5. Place the completed Current Cash Flow form in your "Assets, Debt, Net Worth, Cash Flow" file folder.

6. Acknowledge and praise yourself for your efforts, regardless of what the numbers say. The fact is: You are laying down the foundation upon which you'll increase your wealth and create Financial Freedom.

7. If you don't already have one, open a checking account immediately and use it to pay as many bills as possible.

8. Make an appointment to read chapter 12, "Step 6: Tracking Your Annual Income Records." Write down the appointment and keep it.

CHAPTER *12*

STEP 6: TRACKING YOUR ANNUAL INCOME RECORDS

Sure, you're the all-important President of your own million-dollar company, but even financial giants schmooze once in a while. So let's talk baseball!

In baseball, we keep score by tracking the number of runs made by each team over a certain period of time, called innings. The team that scores the most runs wins.

Successful money management is much the same.

In the money game, you keep score two ways.

- By tracking income and expenses over a certain period of time (usually monthly)
- By tracking assets annually

Setting up your tracking system will probably be the most intensive part of getting started on Your Personal Money Management System.

The good news: You have to set up your tracking system only once. When in place, it's easy to maintain on an ongoing basis. And you'll soon discover that your tracking system will be a *major time-saver* throughout the year.

MANAGEMENT TIP ▚▚▚▚▚▚▚▚▚▚▚▚▚▚▚▚▚▚▚▚▚

You win when you're practicing Financial Freedom and increasing your wealth by at least 10 percent of every month's income.

▚▚▚▚▚▚▚▚▚▚▚▚▚▚▚▚▚▚▚▚▚▚▚▚▚▚▚▚▚▚▚

TRACKING YOUR TWO INCOMES

The first system you'll be setting up will track your income. We'll be working with two types of income: monthly income and asset income.

Monthly income is the money coming to you each month that you use to pay your expenses, *regardless of its source.* (Perhaps you earn $4,000 a month working at a job, or maybe it's interest from a trust fund. Either way, if you use that $4,000 to pay your bills, your monthly income is $4,000.)

Asset income is money earned in your Wealth-Building Account that remains in the account accumulating interest. Asset income is retained rather than spent. It's money that's working for you, growing for your anticipated financial needs and dreams.

Asset income is the opposite of a loan or mortgage. With a loan or mortgage, you buy something now and agree to pay for it later, usually over a specified period of time. By building assets, you pay yourself now for the freedom to buy something you may want later. Loans and mortgages demand that a certain amount of your life's precious energy be expended each month for something already bought. Assets allow you the freedom to invest your energy in trade for an almost infinite number of future choices.

Important note: If you are retired, you probably use the interest from your assets as an important source of monthly income. For you, even though this income is generated from your assets, we'll ask you to treat that part of it you use to pay bills as your monthly income.

Right now, you're probably wondering "Well, what does a tracking system *look* like?"

Tracking systems are often shown on something called a spreadsheet. Don't panic! You don't have to be a certified public accountant to read a spreadsheet. In fact, a spreadsheet is simply a visual display in which the information you're tracking is entered so that you can see it clearly. That's all. No hieroglyphics, no secret codes.

ANNUAL INCOME SUMMARY: THE RICH AND GOLDIE BANKS COMPANY

On page 116 you'll find the Banks Family's Annual Income Summary Spreadsheet, which shows how Rich and Goldie did during the first half of 1993. Let's take a look!

First let's view the big picture.

■ Notice that the spreadsheet is organized by *month*. A month is the amount of time most businesses use to keep score. It's advantages? A month is a convenient time frame, not so long that you lose track or so short that it becomes a burden to keep records.

■ Also notice that the spreadsheet is divided into three sections: "Monthly Income," "Asset Income" and "Keeping Score." (For now we'll be focusing on only two types of income. We'll leave "Keeping Score" for a later chapter.)

Let's first zero in on the monthly income information.

■ In the section called "Monthly Income," check out the column called "Monthly Projections." The figures in this column are Rich and Goldie's best estimate, *based on their 1992 income*, of what they anticipated on average for each month of 1993.

■ Next notice their gross salary of $3,000 (or $36,000 per year). Since Rich and Goldie had been tracking for six months, the "Totals" column at the right side of the spreadsheet shows $18,000 (half of $36,000), which is just what we'd expect. The last column, "Average per Month," shows $3,000 ($18,000 divided by six months). *Keep in mind that this is gross pay, before any deductions are taken.*

■ On the next line down, you can see the results of Rich and Goldie's mail-order business, which had earned a total of $7,800 so far that year, the average being $1,300 per month. The spreadsheet clearly shows how this sideline income varied month to month, while the salary income remained constant.

■ "Other (specify)": Note that this line has $0. That's because

MENTAL TIP ▰▼▼▼▼▼▼▼▼▼▼▼▼▼▼▼▼▼▼▼▼▼▼▼▼▼▼▼▰

 As they say, one picture is worth a thousand words. Seeing your financial information in an organized form, like a spreadsheet, gives your consciousness a clear indication of (1) what is happening to your money and (2) what needs to happen so that you can enjoy positive cash flow and increase your wealth by at least 10 percent of your annual income.

▰▼▼▼▼▼▼▼▼▼▼▼▼▼▼▼▼▼▼▼▼▼▼▼▼▼▼▼▼▼▼▰

Rich and Goldie didn't use any income they may have received from investments, gifts or other sources to finance their monthly standard of living.

■ To summarize, their total income for the first half of 1993 was $25,800. That's an average of $4,300 per month.

Note that Rich and Goldie's actual income was running an average of $200 per month more than what they had projected ($4,300 versus $4,100). By looking at the spreadsheet, Rich and Goldie could see that this was a direct result of an increase in their mail-order business: $1,300 average per month rather than the projected $1,100 per month.

Now let's take a look at Rich and Goldie's asset income.

This portion of the spreadsheet provides a way to regularly track increases in assets. This is vital because increases in your assets are how you become wealthy.

■ As for the "Monthly Income" section, the first column in the "Asset Income" section is a projection, based on the previous year, of how Rich and Goldie anticipated doing in 1993.

■ The first line represents interest accumulating in a bank certificate of deposit (CD), which had originally been funded with $25,000 and had now grown by $2,100. Notice that the monthly average of $166 is less than the projected average of $190 (probably due to a slightly lower interest rate when Rich and Goldie "rolled over" the CD).

■ The second line shows income received from other investments, which is in alignment with what Rich and Goldie projected.

1993 YEAR	MONTHLY PRO-JECTIONS	JAN.	FEB.	MAR.	APR.	MAY
1 MONTHLY INCOME						
2 Gross Salary	3,000	3,000	3,000	3,000	3,000	3,000
3 Mail-Order	1,100	1,300	1,000	1,500	1,400	1,300
4 Other (specify)	0	0	0	0	0	0
5						
6 Totals	4,100	4,300	4,000	4,500	4,400	4,300
7						
8						
9 ASSET INCOME						
10 CD Interest	190	160	165	163	166	169
11 Other Interest	50	49	52	51	52	53
12 Gifts	0	0	0	0	0	0
13 Paid to Myself	167	167	167	167	167	167
14						
15 Totals	407	376	384	381	385	389
16						
17						
18 KEEPING SCORE						
19 Monthly Income						
20 Deductions						
21 Net Income						
22 Personal Expenses						
23 Business Expenses						
24 Monthly Net						
25 Cumulative						
26						
27						
28						
29						
30						

THE BANKS FAMILY'S ANNUAL

■ The next line indicates they received a *gift* of $600 in June. The circumstance: Through a will, Goldie received her late aunt's engagement ring. She chose to convert the ring to cash. The $600 shows up in the "Asset Income" section rather than in the "Monthly Income" section because Rich and Goldie elected to

INCOME SUMMARY SPREADSHEET

JUNE	JULY	AUG.	SEPT.	OCT.	NOV.	DEC.	TOTALS	AVERAGE PER MONTH	
									1
3,000							18,000	3,000	2
1,300							7,800	1,300	3
0							0	0	4
									5
4,300							25,800	4,300	6
									7
									8
									9
173							996	166	10
55							312	52	11
600							600	100	12
167							1,002	167	13
									14
995							2,910	485	15
									16
									17
									18
									19
									20
									21
									22
									23
									24
									25
									26
									27
									28
									29
									30

place the money in their Wealth-Building Account instead of spending it.

■ The line called "Paid to Myself" may be the most important entry of all. It represents the amount of money the Banks family had invested so far that year using their Financial Freedom program. You can see that the figure recorded each month is consistently $167. This is because Rich and Goldie have an individual retirement account (IRA) in which they anticipated placing $2,000 for the year—that is, they would put $167 per month into the IRA.

■ Checking out the "Totals" and "Average per Month" columns at the far right, you can easily see what's happening to the Banks family's asset income. For the first half of the year, Rich and Goldie had increased their wealth by $2,910. If they continued at this rate, they would have wound up the year with $5,820 more than they had at the beginning of the year. Their average per month was $485, more than the $407 they projected. This is clearly attributed to the gift of $600 they received. (Aren't gifts great!)

TAKE THE PLUNGE!

If you turn to page 224, you'll find a blank Annual Income Summary Spreadsheet. Go ahead and fill in the spreadsheet for the current year. Don't forget to refer to the Banks family's spreadsheet as needed for clarification and inspiration. (Important: If you don't have monthly income figures for last year, don't be concerned. Leave the "Monthly Projections" column blank. Next year, you'll be able to use this year's figures for your projections.)

And remember: You're doing great!

MANAGEMENT TIP ▗▼▼▼▼▼▼▼▼▼▼▼▼▼▼▼▼▼▼▼▼▼▼▼▼▼▼▖

The critical decision in keeping track of your annual income is deciding whether you record the money as monthly income or asset income. This decision should be based totally upon how the money will be used, not where it comes from. Foolproof guideline: If you use the money to pay bills, it's monthly income. If you deposit it in your Wealth-Building Account instead of spending it, it's asset income. It's that simple!

▗▼▼▼▼▼▼▼▼▼▼▼▼▼▼▼▼▼▼▼▼▼▼▼▼▼▼▼▼▼▼▼▖

ACTION STEPS 〰〰〰〰〰〰〰〰〰〰〰〰〰〰〰〰

1. Enter your monthly income on your Annual Income Summary Spreadsheet for each month of the current year.

2. Enter your asset income for each month.

3. Calculate your totals and average per month. (Remember to use pencil, since these change from month to month.)

4. If you have monthly projections, check your actual average per month figures against your projections. This way, your Private Access Learning System (PALS) receives the clear information it needs to support you in achieving your goals.

5. Get a new file folder, label it "Annual Income and Expense Records," and place your completed Annual Income Summary Spreadsheet in it.

6. Acknowledge and appreciate yourself! You now have a significant part of your tracking system in place!

7. Make an appointment to read chapter 13, "Step 7: Learning to Keep Your Monthly Expense Records." Write down the appointment and keep it.

CHAPTER *13*

STEP 7: LEARNING TO KEEP YOUR MONTHLY EXPENSE RECORDS

All successful companies have at least one thing in common: *They keep track of how their money is being spent.*

Whenever we suggest that our clients begin keeping track of how they spend their money, we almost always get the same response: Sounds like a great idea, but they don't have a clue as to how to systematically track their spending *easily and efficiently.*

After a bit of thought, most clients will cringe and ask: "You mean we have to write down every penny we spend?"

We usually keep them in bone-chilling suspense for a wicked little moment before we answer: "No, that won't be necessary."

Which brings us to the next question: If we don't recommend writing down every red cent, what *are* our guidelines for the kind of spending you must track to be

successful at money management?

Our answer: You'll have to wait and see. Our experience with human behavior tells us that right now you are probably knee-deep in the following indignant, wonderfully irrational self-talk: "What's with these Hulnick characters?! Why do I have to wait and see? Do they think I'm too stupid to understand? Hey, I bought this book, and I demand to know their guidelines right now!"

Dear reader, a little patience is in order. Before we tell you *what* to track, we think it makes a lot of sense for us to explain what a successful tracking program is and how you can make your tracking system work easily and efficiently. Don't you agree?

THE JOY OF TRACKING

Surprise! Keeping track of your money can be a very simple and satisfying process. That's because once you've put your tracking system in place and gotten into the habit of using it, the actual process of tracking your expenses takes a surprisingly short time.

If one activity is crucial to the success of managing your money, it's regular tracking. We can't imagine how we'd ever be able to do our own financial planning without the information provided by these records.

And believe it or not, many people learn to really enjoy keeping expense records. The part of your mind that's in charge of tracking your money *loves* its job! Our clients who have successful tracking programs report a distinct feeling of satisfaction and empowerment in keeping their records. They compare it to the good feeling you get when you make a list of things to do and cross them off as you do them. (Our own personal experience in tracking our finances matches this sense of enjoyment they describe.)

DEVELOPING A SYSTEM

In chapter 6, "A Quest for Balance," we talked about the importance of the relationship between income and expenses. Our years of financial counseling have taught us a critical lesson: Unless you shift the psychological balance governing your income/expenses, as your income goes up you'll experience a parallel increase in your expenses. To simply focus on creating additional income without carefully monitoring expenses will produce little change in your overall wealth.

Now *that's* a reason for learning to track your expenses if we've ever heard one!

Like your income tracking system, the heart of your expense tracking system involves using spreadsheets. However, this particular spreadsheet is organized according to the kinds of checks you write. It is, in fact, a visual record of every check you write during any given month—and where your money goes.

We've found there's really something magical about keeping an expense record. One of our clients spontaneously stopped smoking after keeping an expense record for only two months. How does something like this happen?

Our theory: When you actually see where your money is going, this new awareness allows your mind to provide you with alternative ideas previously unimagined. In the case of the former smoker, two months of tracking opened her up to this bright idea: If she dumped the butts, she could spend a first-class, sun-drenched week in Hawaii every two years with the savings. After that financial epiphany, it was "Aloha, Marlboro. Hello, Maui!"

MONTHLY EXPENSE RECORDS: THE RICH AND GOLDIE BANKS COMPANY

To give you a closer look at how to use a Monthly Expense Spreadsheet, let's check the records of the Banks family. You'll find Rich and Goldie's expense spreadsheet on page 124.

As you can see, this is the Banks Family's Monthly Expense Spreadsheet for January 1993. On it Rich and Goldie recorded all the pertinent information about the money they spent that month. The record includes: all the checks written in January, the dates they were written, the check numbers, to whom the checks were written and the amount of each check (logged in the appropriate column for the category of expenditure).

Are you ready to get into the nitty-gritty of keeping track of what you—and the Banks family—spend each month? Let's go!

If you want to develop some spreadsheet savvy, here's what to look for.

The most important column of all. The first thing to notice on the Banks family's spreadsheet is column 1, "Pay Yourself First." Since the primary aim of your corporation is to provide abundantly for you and your family, *the most important check you'll write each month is the one to yourself.* Clients frequently ask if we advise actually writing a check to themselves each month and depositing it in a separate Wealth-Building Account. *As we've said, we think it's essential.* Having a separate account is a clear and wonderful way to monitor how your company's assets are growing. As you can see from their spreadsheet, Rich and Goldie had opened an individual retirement account (IRA) at First Bank. They paid themselves $167 this month.

The family's expenditures. Columns 2 through 12 are organized according to the types of expenses Rich and Goldie pay out monthly, from mortgage to phone to entertainment.

Expenses that aren't monthly. Some items you pay for on an occasional basis rather than as part of your regular monthly routine. For example, in January Rich and Goldie purchased a birthday gift for a friend. This one-time expense: $28.40. They also made a donation to their church. This yearly payment: $40. Each of these expenditures doesn't require a column of its own. Instead, they're listed in column 13, "Miscellaneous," along with other expenses that aren't routine.

Cash or check? When we counsel clients about keeping financial records, they inevitably ask us the following questions.

"Is it better to pay by cash or check?"

"And when I do pay by cash, what's the best way to keep track of these expenditures?"

Our answers: The main advantage of writing checks is that your canceled check is both a *receipt* and a *written record* of an expenditure. Most people find it's easier to keep accurate records of monthly expenses if they use checks for most of their purchases.

However, many people like to use cash occasionally, particularly when the expense is small. No one wants to write a check for every parking lot he enters, every magazine he buys, every candy bar he sneaks on his diet. It's just not practical.

Here's the way we suggest you keep track of small expenses paid by cash: *Write one check each month for petty cash.*

You determine the amount of this check by "guesstimating" two factors: (1) how much you need each month to pay for the "small stuff"; and (2) how much "mystery money" you're willing

THE BANKS FAMILY'S MONTHLY

	DATE	CHECK #	TO	1 PAY YOURSELF FIRST (10% MINIMUM)	2 FOOD	3 RENT OR MORTGAGE	4 CLOTHES	5 LAUNDRY
1	2	234	Home Loan Assoc.			860.00		
2	3	235	Sam's Market		125.80			
3	4	236	Petty Cash					
4	6	237	White's Service Station					
5	7	238	So. State Utilities					
6	7	239	Star Cleaners					33.80
7	7	240	The Natural Gas Co.					
8	13	241	Dr. Sam Jones					
9	14	242	Master Bank Credit Card				52.40	
10	15	243	Happy Day School					
11	15	244	Sam's Market		147.10			
12	15	245	White's Service Station					
13	16	246	First Bank Credit Card		48.30			
14	19	247	Universal Phone Co.					
15	19	248	Youngtown Clothes				Kids 54.10	
16	22	249	Presents, Inc.					
17	23	250	United Church					
18	24	251	Jack's Finance Co.					
19	25	252	Dr. U. Getwell					
20	25	253	Henry Good (loan-parents)					
21	25	254	Robinson's Dept. Store					
22	25	255	Our Accrual Account					
23								
24								
25	27	256	Sam's Market		117.40			
26	29	257	First Bank-IRA	167.00				
27								
28								
29								
30								
			TOTALS	167.00	438.60	860.00	106.50	33.80

to let "slip through the cracks" without knowing where it went. This check is then recorded just like any other check in your Monthly Expense Spreadsheet.

For example, let's see how the Banks family handled this situation on its spreadsheet. Rich and Goldie had decided to keep $150

Month <u>JANUARY</u> Year <u>1993</u>

EXPENSE SPREADSHEET

6 MEDICAL	7 KIDS' SCHOOL/ CHILD CARE	8 AUTO & GASOLINE	9 PHONE & UTILITIES	10 ACCRUALS	11 ENTER- TAINMENT	12 PERSONAL CARE	13 MISCEL- LANEOUS	14 TOTAL	15 DEDUCT	
								860.00	✓	1
								125.80		2
							Petty Cash 150.00	150.00		3
		Gas 24.60						24.60		4
			Electric 79.20					79.20		5
								33.80		6
			Gas 20.00					20.00		7
95.00								95.00		8
					63.00	32.00	Min. Pymt. 15.00	162.40		9
	190.00							190.00		10
								147.10		11
		Repair 105.90						105.90		12
						32.15	Min. Pymt. 24.00	104.45		13
			Phone 123.30					123.30		14
								54.10		15
							Gift 28.40	28.40		16
							Donation 40.00	40.00		17
		Loan 140.00						140.00		18
160.00								160.00		19
							50.00	50.00		20
							Min. Pymt. 50.00	50.00		21
		{	Property Taxes–150.00 }					375.00		22
		{	Auto Insurance–185.00 }							23
		{	Life Insurance–40.00 }							24
								117.40		25
								167.00		26
										27
										28
										29
										30
255.00	190.00	270.50	222.50	375.00	63.00	64.15	357.40	3,403.45		

in cash on hand each month. So if you check their spreadsheet, you'll see that they wrote a check to petty cash on January 4, 1993 (check 236). They entered this expense under the "Miscellaneous" category (column 13).

If you choose to use the petty cash approach, be sure that your monthly check for petty cash is truly petty (as in *insignificant*) in relation to your overall expenses. For example, if your monthly expenses are $3,000 and you're writing checks for petty cash in the amount of $1,000, that represents one-third of your entire monthly expenses. That's not our idea of "petty cash."

To be successful at managing your money with ease and efficiency, we suggest you develop a better way to keep track of what you're spending. One good way: Begin paying the larger bills represented within that $1,000 by check.

Some people, however, like to pay for almost everything in cash. That's fine—as long as you realize it's *essential* to keep track of your expenses in a way that supports Your Personal Money Management System. And that means consistently getting receipts for all your cash purchases and expenses every month. It also means remembering in which jacket pocket you shoved them. And after you find them, it means entering these cash expenditures on your Monthly Expense Spreadsheet in the same way you enter your checks.

MENTAL TIP ▰▼▼▼▼▼▼▼▼▼▼▼▼▼▼▼▼▼▼▼▼▼▼▼▼▼▼▼▼▼▰

For years, we've been doing something with our monthly petty cash allotment that increases our sense of abundance and self-esteem and, well, is just plain fun. Each week, we take $5 from petty cash and put it in an envelope. At the end of the year, the envelope is filled with $260 we've saved. What do we do with the money? We certainly don't pay the electric bill with it. No sirree! We treat ourselves to a lavish dinner to celebrate our wedding anniversary. Think about it. Does going to an elegant restaurant and ordering anything you want for dinner, regardless of price, have the effect of raising or lowering your experience of wealth? Try an exercise in luxury like our once-a-year, over-the-top dinner and see if it increases your consciousness of wealth. We bet it does!

▲▲▲▲▲▲▲▲▲▲▲▲▲▲▲▲▲▲▲▲▲▲▲▲▲▲▲▲▲▲▲▲▲▲▲▲▲▲

Our own personal rule of thumb: We pay cash only for expenses that are small enough to come out of our monthly allotment for petty cash. Everything else we pay by check or credit card.

There are a few more things in the Banks Family's Monthly Expense Spreadsheet that we'd like to point out.

Tracking tax deductions. Notice column 15, "Deduct." This is the information you'll be glad you have when tax time rolls around, especially if you itemize expenses rather than taking the standard deduction. Either way, you simply place a check mark next to the items that are tax deductible. *Imagine:* No more shoe boxes filled with receipts waiting to be sorted on April 14! No more envelopes stuffed with a mishmash of papers demanding to be organized!

Of course, to complete this column you may have to start by finding out the answer to this question: "What expenses do I have that are tax deductible?" Since the guidelines governing deductions can vary from year to year and from situation to situation, we suggest that you check with your tax preparer. After you've completed your own Monthly Expense Spreadsheet, show it to your tax preparer and ask her which items you should single out for purposes of preparing your tax returns.

If you look at Rich and Goldie's tax deductions for January, you'll see that they checked their mortgage payment. Other possible types of deductions include property taxes, certain moving expenses, charitable contributions and certain medical expenses.

There's a good reason to keep track of tax deductions: It saves you money! When tax season comes around and everyone else is paying his accountant by the hour to straighten out expense records, yours will already be in top-notch shape—because you have a built-in way of tracking deductible expenses. Your accountant's fee will be minimal, since all she'll really need to do is transfer the figures directly from your records to the computer tax form. The first time we took our records to our accountant to use in preparing our taxes, he was so impressed that he offered us a job in his firm!

Credit card payments. Entering a credit card payment on your spreadsheet is a "special case" scenario. Why? Even though you're writing *one check*, you're usually paying for *several items*, each of

MANAGEMENT TIP ▚▼▼▼▼▼▼▼▼▼▼▼▼▼▼▼▼▼▼▼▼▼▼▜

If you use credit cards a lot, it may be easier to create a mini-spreadsheet for each bill. Then you simply enter the total for each category on your Monthly Expense Spreadsheet.

▚▼▼▼▼▼▼▼▼▼▼▼▼▼▼▼▼▼▼▼▼▼▼▼▼▼▼▼▼▜

which might belong in a *different column.*

For example, take a look at Rich and Goldie's entry on line 9—check 242, dated January 14, to Master Bank Credit Card.

What you see listed is: $52.40 in the "Clothes" category, $63 under "Entertainment," $32 under "Personal Care" and $15 in the "Miscellaneous" column.

How did Rich and Goldie come up with these amounts?

First they added together all the items on the Master Bank bill that were purchased in each category listed on their spreadsheet. Then they entered each of those total amounts in the proper column.

For example, the $63 listed under "Entertainment" (column 11) might represent only one purchase: two tickets to a Garth Brooks concert ($63 charged to the Hollywood Bowl). However, it just as well could be charges to several merchants: Dim Sum Restaurant ($22), Blockbuster Video ($12.50) and Tower Records ($28.50). If that's the case, it's still added together as *the total spent for entertainment that month.*

Finally, Rich and Goldie entered the sum of all the individual columns, $162.40, under "Total" (column 14). Then they wrote their check to the credit card company for this amount.

Important note: Notice the "Miscellaneous" category (column 13). Above the $15 entry is the notation "min. pymt." This is short for "minimum monthly payment." To understand the reason for this entry, we need to remember that the Banks family had an outstanding balance of $464 on its Master Bank card, which required a minimum monthly payment of $15.

There are several strategies for paying off credit card bills. One is to pay all current charges *plus* the amount of the minimum monthly payment. This is what Rich and Goldie are doing with their Master Bank card. In this way, they keep up-to-date with current purchases while at the same time whittling away at the unpaid balance.

A faster method for paying off a credit card bill is to divide the unpaid balance into ten equal payments. Each month, pay all current purchases plus one-tenth (10 percent) of the unpaid balance. Whichever method you choose, if you're going to use credit cards, it's essential that you pay for all current purchases each month when the bill is due. *Otherwise, you will not have accurate information to place on your Monthly Expense Spreadsheet.*

For Rich and Goldie, 10 percent would be $46.40 a month. Using this approach, they'd pay off the card in ten months.

So the formula for paying down credit cards is: card purchases plus card interest plus a portion of the unpaid balance.

No more shock over unexpected bills. Another extremely important part of your Monthly Expense Spreadsheet is column 10, "Accruals." Why? Some bills, such as property taxes, certain types of insurance premiums and estimated income taxes, are paid not monthly but only once every three, four or even six months. The accrual process makes it easier to handle these large non-monthly expenses by spreading them evenly over the year. But unless you plan for these large expenses, you risk being financially overwhelmed when they unexpectedly come due to be paid.

The way you plan for these bills is by opening an accrual account and paying money into it monthly. *Example:* Even though you're not billed for your property tax each month, you still deposit a payment in your accrual account every month so that the money is accumulating (or *accruing*) over a period of months until the bill is actually due. Then when the time comes, you have the money to pay a hefty bill. (No more moaning "How will I ever make it through this month with all these unexpected bills?")

Built-in accuracy system. Another important feature of this spreadsheet is what we call a double-entry system. (*Note:* We're *not* referring to a traditional bookkeeping method called double entry, which deals with debts and credits.) Our double-entry system simply means that *you enter the amount of each check twice.*

The first entry: Place the amount in the appropriate category that tells what kind of expense it is. (On the Banks family's spreadsheet, these would be columns 1 through 13.)

The second entry: Place the amount in the next-to-last column, "Total." (On the Banks family's spreadsheet, this is column 14).

Example: Let's look at how Rich and Goldie kept track of their mortgage payment on the spreadsheet. Their check to the Home Loan Association in the amount of $860 is listed under column 3, "Rent or Mortgage." Notice that they also recorded the $860 in column 14, "Total." (In a moment, we'll explain just how this provides you with a way to be sure your records are correct. For now, simply be aware that it's part of the spreadsheet.)

What's the bottom line? Okay, it's the end of the month. You've systematically recorded your expenses for the last four weeks. Besides standing in awe of your achievement, what do you do next? (No, you don't call up the *Wall Street Journal* and tell them the news.)

Hint: If a little birdie just whispered the word "total" in your ear, you're right on the money, especially if your first response was "I have the unstoppable urge to add up all the columns on my spreadsheet!"

Let's look at how the Banks family computed the totals for its monthly expense records. First Rich and Goldie added up the entries in each individual category (columns 1 through 13). On the bottom line of the spreadsheet, marked "Totals," they entered the sum for each category. *For example:* To calculate the monthly expense for food (column 2), they added up four entries ($125.80, $147.10, $48.30 and $117.40). Then they entered this sum ($438.60) at the bottom of column 2.

They did this process for all 13 categories of expenses. When they were finished, they had total amounts for each of the categories in the boxes on the bottom line of their spreadsheet.

The double-entry accuracy test. Now Rich and Goldie were down to the wire. They added together all the total amounts listed for columns 1 through 13. *This sum should equal the amount in the "Total" column (Rich and Goldie's column 14).* This is the double-entry system we referred to that lets you test the accuracy of your work. In Rich and Goldie's case, the two totals matched. Their January expenses were $3,403.45. If their two totals *don't* match, they know they've made a mathematical error and need to carefully check their work.

MANAGEMENT TIP ▗▚▚▚▚▚▚▚▚▚▚▚▚▚▚▚▚▚▚▚▚▚▚▚▚▚▚

 We suggest that you open a separate checking account for accrual payments. We discovered this from counseling clients who are just learning about accruals: It's important to actually transfer the money from your regular checking account into your special accrual account. Those clients who didn't often got to the end of the month thinking that they had more money to spend than they actually did. (Sound familiar?) A separate accrual account will help keep you on track.

HOW TO CUSTOMIZE YOUR EXPENSE RECORDS

Having your very own expense records is an *invaluable* tool in managing your money. For example, here are three important ways in which these records can help you.

1. You always know just where your money is going.
2. You can project how much extra money you'll have at the end of the year.
3. Most important of all: You are conscious of your spending habits.

As you begin to see the positive results of keeping expense records, you'll find, as we have, that the entire process of money management becomes exciting and fun!

So let's get started on personalizing your Monthly Expense Spreadsheet.

When working with your Monthly Expense Spreadsheet, the first step is to set up your column headings, or categories. Since the total number of columns on the spreadsheet is 15, you'll want to have a maximum of 15 categories. This includes one column each for miscellaneous, totals, accruals, deductible expenses and that most important column—"Pay Yourself First"!

This leaves ten columns for you to categorize your expenses according to your personal situation. (Some people find that ten categories is not enough, and they use two spreadsheets each month.)

If, like Rich and Goldie Banks, you operate a small sideline business, we suggest you use one spreadsheet for personal expenses and one for business expenses.

But our most important recommendation is: Experiment! Discover what works for you and do it!

Here are the things to be aware of as you're setting up your records.

Choosing your categories. Many people feel confused, uncertain or inadequate about figuring out what categories will work best for them. Our experience has shown us that these feelings are often unconscious *resistance* by people who are frightened to face the truth about how they've managed money. Why? Because they're busy judging themselves as "stupid ninnies who deserve a kick in the pants." Who'd want to face that music?

Remember our attorney client, Elizabeth? She taught us our first law of the psychodynamics between people and their money: *Some people are in complete denial about the state of their finances simply because they're afraid to look at the facts.* The process of selecting your categories for a Monthly Expense Spreadsheet is one of the "trigger points" for choosing *awareness* over denial, *empowerment* over fear.

This process—and the choice you make—is critically important to the success of Your Personal Money Management System. It's so important that we've developed two worksheets to make the process of category selection flow *easily and efficiently.* We're sure these forms will take the sting out of this big step in your mastery of money management. (These forms are on pages 226 and 227.)

The difference between the two forms: One contains specific categories that fit most people's life situations. The other is *blank* so that you can enter any categories that fit your unique situation.

Notice that the worksheet that lists specific categories (on page 226) is divided into two sections: "Monthly Fixed Expenses" and "Monthly Variable Expenses." Fixed expenses are easier to plan for, since you know they'll be the same each month. Variable expenses, by definition, are not necessarily the same month to month. These are the expenses that require more careful monitoring.

Use your canceled checks: To make maximum use of Your Worksheets for Monthly Expense Categories, gather your canceled checks, check stubs or check records for *the past three months.* (We suggest you go through three months so that you'll have a thorough sampling of the checks you write each month.)

Then proceed through your checks, placing a check mark in column 1 of the appropriate category on the worksheet ("Mortgage/Rent," "Health Insurance," "Utilities," "Groceries" and so forth). Don't be concerned about whom the check was made payable to or how much it was for. You're interested only in assigning it a category.

When you come to a canceled check for a category in which you've already made a check mark, just place another mark in column 2. If you come to a canceled check that doesn't fit any of the categories, simply create a new category on the blank form and place a mark next to it in column 1. *Note:* All checks in the same category do *not* have to be written to the same person or business. For example, maybe you've bought food from several different markets. All those purchases are entered in the same category, labeled "Groceries."

The only exception to this method: Checks made out for credit card purchases must be handled differently. To accurately categorize these expenses, you'll need to either (1) retrieve the past few months of credit card bills and see what specific purchases are included on the bills or (2) if you're well acquainted with the kinds of items you charge on your credit cards, simply use that information when choosing your categories.

Let's say you've finished listing your categories and you discover that you have more than the standard 15 (10 *plus* columns for miscellaneous, totals, accruals, deductible expenses and "Pay Yourself First"). What do you do? Simple. You can combine more than one category in a single column. For example, you might combine "Mortgage/Rent" with "Utilities." Or maybe "Mortgage/Rent" with "Utilities" and "Furnishings." The important thing is to combine categories within which you write only a few checks. (Of course, you can always use an additional spreadsheet, as we've already pointed out.)

The good news: Yes, this process will take a little time, but *you'll need to do it only once* to get your expense records started.

So go ahead and establish your categories! (And keep your canceled checks handy for the next part of this process.)

SETTING UP YOUR SPREADSHEET

As we've said, setting up your Monthly Expense Spreadsheet can be the most challenging aspect of getting started on Your Personal Money Management System. So if you find yourself wondering whether this is really such a "good time" to start or not, remind yourself why you purchased this book in the first place: *Your life will be much better when you're living with greater Financial Freedom and the wealth it generates.*

In other words, just do it!

And here's what to do: Now that you've determined your categories, we'll explain the two choices you have in setting up your spreadsheet. The first choice will work best for you if you'd like to have a super-clear picture of your current total expenses.

Regardless of which choice you make, you'll need a blank Monthly Expense Spreadsheet, which you'll find on page 228. Notice that the spreadsheet has 30 lines, so if you write more than 30 checks each month, you'll need to use extra sheets.

Read over both choices for setting up your spreadsheet and then decide which method will work best for you.

Choice 1. Write the name of each category at the top of a spreadsheet column. Now go back three months and begin entering each check in its appropriate column, along with the amount of the check. Remember, do this for *every* check in the three-month period, using one or more Monthly Expense Spreadsheets, as needed. Calculate your totals for each month. For most

MENTAL TIP ▰▼▼▼▼▼▼▼▼▼▼▼▼▼▼▼▼▼▼▼▼▼▼▼▼▼▼▼▼▼▰

 When you've completed setting up your Monthly Expense Spreadsheet, take time to reward yourself. Remember the importance of acknowledging and appreciating yourself every time you successfully complete a step toward your goal of establishing your Financial Freedom program. It's vital to complete the psychological cycle by positively reinforcing the success you've achieved. This sets you up for your next success!

▲▲▲▲▲▲▲▲▲▲▲▲▲▲▲▲▲▲▲▲▲▲▲▲▲▲▲▲▲▲▲▲▲

people, Choice 1 works best. Believe us, it's more than worth the extra time to get a clear picture of where your money is going. (And if you want an even clearer picture, do four, five or even six months' worth of checks.)

Choice 2. Write the name of each category at the top of a column and enter your checks, starting at the beginning of *the current month*. While this method is shorter, it's best used only if you already have a good idea of your expense picture.

ACTION STEPS

1. Gather your canceled checks, check stubs or check records. Use Your Worksheets for Monthly Expense Categories as a guide to establish the kinds of expenses for your lifestyle.

2. Enter your categories on the Monthly Expense Spreadsheet.

3. Determine the expenditures for which you want to establish accruals.

4. Open a separate checking account for accruals.

5. Open a Wealth-Building Account in which you deposit your "Pay Yourself First" checks.

6. Complete a Monthly Expense Spreadsheet for each month of the current year using a minimum of three months.

7. If you have a small business, consider setting up one Monthly Expense Spreadsheet for personal expenses and one for business expenses.

8. Get a new file folder, label it "Monthly Expense Records," and place all the forms you worked with in this chapter into it.

9. You've now completed nearly 75 percent of your tracking system. Acknowledge yourself for your progress.

10. Make an appointment with yourself to read chapter 14, "Step 8: Preparing Your Annual Expense Records." Write down the appointment and keep it.

CHAPTER *14*

STEP 8: PREPARING YOUR ANNUAL EXPENSE RECORDS

Bet you've had an experience like this.

You're walking by a department store when you spot a jacket in the window. But not just *any* jacket. This one's got *your* name on it. You know, it's your favorite color, your favorite style, your favorite material— and best of all, it's on sale.

You've just got to have it!

Your thought process would probably go something like this: "Wow, that's really nice. Let's see how much it is. Yipes! That's a lot of money for a jacket. On the other hand, it is on sale, and I love it. What if I wait too long and it's not on sale anymore? I'll have missed a great deal. But I don't really know if I can afford to buy it right now. Oh, gosh! What should I do?"

Does any of this angst sound familiar?

If so, here comes Your Personal Money Management System to the rescue!

Once you're maintaining your annual expense

records, that shaky shopping scenario can sound like

this instead: "Wow, that's really a nice jacket. Let's see how much it is. Yipes! That's a lot of money for a jacket. But it is on sale. Let me think a minute. Last month I was slightly under my clothing expenditure for the month. And I haven't used any of this month's allotted clothing fund so far. Yes, the jacket is expensive, but I love it, and I'm going to buy it. That means I'll have to be careful how much I spend on clothes for the rest of this month. And because I've been keeping track, I know exactly how careful I need to be."

As you see, vagueness and uncertainty have been replaced with clarity and knowledge. You know precisely where you are financially, what your options are and what the consequences of your decision will be.

In order for you to arrive at this comfortable and easy understanding of your personal finances, however, we have to introduce you to one more form: the Annual Expense Summary Spreadsheet. It will take a little effort to get the system set up (don't worry, we'll walk you through step-by-step), but it's more than worth it. Once you're keeping these records, you'll always know *exactly* where you stand with respect to any category of spending. Having this comprehensive information at your fingertips makes it much easier to complete the year knowing you will be increasing your wealth by at least 10 percent of your income.

The power of this approach is that unawareness is replaced with precise knowledge. And when your new knowledge is accompanied by behaviors that match your goals, you set up a new "cruise control" in your consciousness. That means that eventually, living in positive cash flow can indeed become your new habit.

SPREADSHEETS AS FRIENDS

Most people find the Annual Expense Summary Spreadsheet to be their most valuable ally in keeping their financial goals crystal clear.

Its main purpose is to provide an overview of your spending month by month. You'll be using this sheet regularly to make decisions about buying things. That's because it gives you concise information on exactly where you stand with your money *and* the financial impact of any purchase.

The good news is that your Annual Expense Summary Spreadsheet is the easiest spreadsheet of all to complete. The reason? All the information for it already exists. You take the figures directly from the Monthly Expense Spreadsheet that you've already prepared. That means no excavating through your canceled checks, no figuring out categories, no monthly calculations. You just copy the information you need from one sheet to the other. What could be simpler?

ANNUAL EXPENSE RECORDS: THE RICH AND GOLDIE BANKS COMPANY

To see how this can work for you, let's first check in with Rich and Goldie and see how it works for them. On page 140 you'll find a record of the Banks family's expenses for the first half of 1993. There are a couple of important things going on here.

■ The months of the year are recorded across the top of the spreadsheet.

This is a tip-off that Rich and Goldie are tracking information from month to month (just as they did on their Annual Income Summary Spreadsheet).

■ In the column marked "Category," each line corresponds to a category that Rich and Goldie already established on their Monthly Expense Spreadsheet (page 124).

They simply entered the totals from their Monthly Expense Spreadsheet directly onto the Annual Expense Summary Spreadsheet in the corresponding categories.

For example, let's look at their medical expenses for January. Checking their Monthly Expense Spreadsheet for January, you can see all these expenses listed in column 6, "Medical." According to their records, Rich and Goldie wrote two checks in the "Medical" category that month: $95 to Dr. Sam Jones on January 13 and $160 to Dr. U. Getwell on January 25. Their monthly total of $255 is entered at the bottom of the "Medical" column.

This is the monthly total that's copied onto the Annual Expense Summary Spreadsheet.

How did Rich and Goldie know exactly where to enter this *monthly* total on the *Annual Expense* Summary Spreadsheet?

By asking two simple questions.

■ What category? (Answer: Medical)
■ What month? (Answer: January)

To see the results of this easy inquiry, check the Banks Family's Annual Expense Summary Spreadsheet. What's entered in the "Medical" category (line 6) for the month of January?

Presto! There's the magic number: $255.

■ You'll notice that "Pay Yourself First" is printed at the top of the list on the Annual Expense Summary Spreadsheet. And it's there for a reason.

We've done this to stress how all-important this practice is for mastering money management. The amount of money listed in this category is the clearest indicator that you're becoming wealthier each month.

Remember: 10 percent of all you earn is yours to keep!

■ Every category should have its own line on the Annual Expense Summary Spreadsheet.

Earlier we told you that if you needed to conserve space, you could combine categories with only one expense per month on your Monthly Expense Spreadsheet.

For instance, on the Banks Family's Monthly Expense Spreadsheet for January, Rich and Goldie combined phone and utilities (column 9), since they receive only one bill per month from each. Rich and Goldie paid three different bills in January that they logged in this category: electric—$79.20; gas—$20; and phone—$123.30.

However, Rich and Goldie used separate lines for each expense on their Annual Expense Summary Spreadsheet. As an example, look at the category entries on lines 11, 12 and 13, and you'll see that Rich and Goldie recorded "Phone," "Utilities (gas)" and "Utilities (electric)" separately. If you take a look at the entries under "January" for these categories, you'll find the amounts were transferred directly from the Banks Family's Monthly Expense Spreadsheet.

■ Next look at the "Monthly Projections" column. Remember that the monthly projections are guidelines, not rigid rules.

These figures represent estimates the Banks family projected based on the previous year's actual expenses. If these figures are going to be helpful, they must be monthly projections that Rich and Goldie think they can realistically adhere to. As estimates, they are not set in stone. The actual expenses will vary. Expenses in certain categories tend to be up one month and down in other months.

THE BANKS FAMILY'S ANNUAL

1993 YEAR CATEGORY	MONTHLY PRO-JECTIONS	JAN.	FEB.	MAR.	APR.	MAY
1 Pay Yourself First	167.00	167.00	167.00	167.00	167.00	167.00
2 Food/Groceries	400.00	438.60	405.00	379.00	390.00	375.00
3 Mortgage	860.00	860.00	860.00	860.00	860.00	860.00
4 Clothes	80.00	106.50	72.20	49.80	75.10	63.90
5 Laundry	30.00	33.80	35.80	46.50	29.30	36.80
6 Medical	200.00	255.00	210.20	170.60	190.20	195.00
7 Child Care	150.00	190.00	150.00	140.00	180.00	120.00
8 Gasoline	100.00	24.60	89.10	76.30	62.80	91.40
9 Auto Repairs	50.00	105.90	0	63.10	0	124.00
10 Auto Loans	140.00	140.00	140.00	140.00	140.00	140.00
11 Phone	100.00	123.30	110.40	98.60	94.80	106.90
12 Utilities (gas)	20.00	20.00	22.40	20.90	19.60	18.40
13 Utilities (electric)	80.00	79.20	97.20	90.40	72.10	67.30
14 Accrue (property tax)	150.00	150.00	150.00	150.00	150.00	150.00
15 Accrue (auto insurance)	185.00	185.00	185.00	185.00	185.00	185.00
16 Accrue (life insurance)	40.00	40.00	40.00	40.00	40.00	40.00
17 Entertainment	50.00	63.00	57.40	36.10	42.50	38.70
18 Personal Care	50.00	64.15	50.00	69.40	50.00	59.60
19 Petty Cash	150.00	150.00	150.00	150.00	150.00	150.00
20 Gifts	20.00	28.40	0	0	22.10	37.60
21 Donations	30.00	40.00	15.00	20.00	30.00	15.00
22 Furnishings	25.00	0	77.10	11.00	0	13.20
23 Debt Repayment	150.00	139.00	160.00	120.00	150.00	130.00
24 Miscellaneous	25.00	0	16.30	21.10	0	14.00
25						
26						
27						
28						
29						
30						
TOTALS	3,252.00	3,403.45	3,260.10	3,104.80	3,100.50	3,198.80

The Big Pay-Off: If Rich and Goldie succeeded in spending within the limits of their monthly projections, the Banks family will have been *wealthier* at the end of the year.

■ The "Miscellaneous" line is used to record "once in a blue moon" expenses.

EXPENSE SUMMARY SPREADSHEET

JUNE	JULY	AUG.	SEPT.	OCT.	NOV.	DEC.	TOTALS	AVERAGE PER MONTH	
167.00							1,002.00	167.00	1
410.00							2,397.60	399.60	2
860.00							5,160.00	860.00	3
86.40							453.90	75.65	4
40.10							222.30	37.05	5
215.60							1,236.60	206.10	6
90.00							870.00	145.00	7
78.20							422.40	70.40	8
38.10							331.10	55.00	9
140.00							840.00	140.00	10
104.10							638.10	106.35	11
18.30							119.60	19.93	12
69.20							475.40	79.25	13
150.00							900.00	150.00	14
185.00							1,110.00	185.00	15
40.00							240.00	40.00	16
90.20							327.90	54.65	17
73.10							366.25	61.05	18
150.00							900.00	150.00	19
0							88.10	14.70	20
25.00							145.00	24.00	21
0							101.30	16.90	22
0							699.00	116.50	23
7.50							58.90	9.80	24
									25
									26
									27
									28
									29
									30
3,037.80							19,105.45	3,184.00	

If you check the Banks Family's Monthly Expense Spreadsheet for January, you'll see that Rich and Goldie have a "Miscellaneous" category (column 13) for several expenses that month: petty cash, minimum credit card payments, gifts and donations. However, these charges were not entered as miscellaneous on

MANAGEMENT TIP ▮▾▾▾▾▾▾▾▾▾▾▾▾▾▾▾▾▾▾▾▾▾▾▾▾▾▾▮

Watch for patterns or trends in all areas of your spending. If you notice a trend to spend more money than you've projected, sound the alarms! It's time to regroup because you could be headed for financial disaster. Our years of financial counseling have shown us that when people begin a trend of spending more than they've projected, the first place they start to cut back is in the "Pay Yourself First" category. Big mistake! This is the last place we suggest you tamper with. When you take money away from your Wealth-Building Account to cover overspending, you're reinforcing a negative habit. You also erode the wealth you've accumulated. And you send your Private Access Learning System (PALS) confusing, mixed messages: "Let's get wealthy, but let's spend money instead of saving it." If this trend goes uncontrolled, your final destination is *debt*.

▮▾▾▾▾▾▾▾▾▾▾▾▾▾▾▾▾▾▾▾▾▾▾▾▾▾▾▾▾▾▾▾▮

their Annual Expense Summary Spreadsheet. Instead, each of these items has its own line listed by category.

Why?

Even though these expenses don't have their own columns on the Banks Family's Monthly Expense Spreadsheet (for reasons of space), they do occur with regularity. Just check the Annual Expense Summary Spreadsheet, and you'll see that the Banks family spent money in each of these categories every month between January and June. For Rich and Goldie to keep track of their money, they must see how much they're spending in each of these categories each month as well as in the "regular" categories. Therefore, each of the categories now has its own line on the annual spreadsheet.

The "Miscellaneous" category is for expenses that rarely occur. For example, a parking ticket you get on a summer vacation. Or a 20-gallon aquarium with two tropical fish named Archie and Edith. More than a few hundred dollars is an indicator that you're not keeping close-enough tabs on your hard-earned money.

FOOD FOR THOUGHT

Here's another example of how you can use the Annual Expense Summary Spreadsheet to help you manage your money. To see how this works, let's look in on the Banks family once again. Let's say it's August 1993, and Rich and Goldie have just decided to have a family reunion at their home over Thanksgiving weekend in November.

Then they begin to worry. How can they possibly plan for this extra food expense and still stay on track with their goal of saving at least 10 percent of their income by year's end?

Solution: First Rich and Goldie add up their food expenses for the six months, from January through June ($2,397.60, according to their spreadsheet). Then they divide the total by six months. This tells them their family has spent an average of $399.60 per month for food. Next they compare this information with their monthly projection for food ($400). *The result:* They immediately know that their expenses are just what they had projected.

What's the value of this precise knowledge?

Rich and Goldie now know they have no "breathing room" left over from the first six months of the year. So they must do careful financial planning from August through October to allow for a surplus in November to cover the Thanksgiving expenses. Rich and Goldie have the advantage of knowing exactly where they stand and what choices are available. They don't have to guess. They know precisely what they must do to stay on course with their wealth-building goals for the year.

By using this very same approach in any category of expense, you can immediately determine how much you've spent so far and how much is realistically available so that you can stay within the range that will result in increasing your wealth that year.

A key to success: Understand that what you've spent in past months and in the current month simply tells you what you can spend next month.

The power of this spreadsheet is that everything is revealed and can readily be evaluated. For example, for January through June, the Banks family's average spending per month was $3,184. That's an average of $68 per month *less* than their monthly projection. At first glance, this looks like a rosy picture. However, if you look closer, you'll see that Rich and Goldie paid an average of only $116.50 a month to reduce their debts. They had projected reducing their debts by $150 every month. A wise move in personal money management would have been for Rich and Goldie to spend an additional $33.50 on reducing their debt, bringing their monthly debt reduction payments to $150. Not only would they have still been within their monthly projection, but by deflecting more interest payments, they would be wealthier at the end of the year.

WEIGHING IN AND SCALING DOWN

Success in money management requires knowledge of this equation: To *increase* spending in one category, you must *decrease* spending in another category or a combination of categories.

It works just like the body weight maintenance program we're on. We both know what our normal weights are. We each weigh ourselves every morning. Generally, we eat two healthy, balanced meals a day, interspersed with fruits and grains, such as Wasa crackers. This keeps us at our normal weights.

However, on special occasions—such as our anniversary splurge—we eat whatever we want, from beluga caviar to Chateaubriand to raspberry cheesecake. The next morning, each of us weighs two or three pounds more. No problem! We simply go back to our regular way of eating, except we cut back *slightly* for a few days until our weights are back to normal.

The moral of the story? What we eat today determines what we *must* eat tomorrow, if we are to maintain our normal weights.

In exactly the same way, what we spend today determines what we *can* spend tomorrow, if we are to maintain our financial goal of always increasing our wealth.

Our weight doctor is fond of saying "Nothing tastes as good as being thin feels."

Similarly, we say that *nothing you will ever buy feels as good as knowing you're debt-free and growing wealthier every day.*

SETTING UP YOUR SPREADSHEET

You'll find your blank Annual Expense Summary Spreadsheet on page 230. You'll need two to begin. One of them is for your "official" tracking of the year's spending. The other is for you to use as a worksheet for gathering specific information we're about to discuss with you.

Because we know this form is *so important to your financial success,* we've developed three different methods for setting up your spreadsheet. Our purpose is to provide you with a method that you're capable of following, no matter what your level of financial record keeping to date.

All three methods work. Which one you choose depends upon several variables. The *most* important: how complete your past record keeping system is, and how much time and energy you're willing to invest.

As we've said, all the methods work. The important thing is to *choose one and do it!*

The Experience Counts Method. *Recommended for:* people with experience working with their finances, adequate past records and a willingness to invest time and energy in the process.

Advantage: maximum financial information.

Disadvantage: maximum expenditure of time and energy.

How it works: Use one copy of the Annual Expense Summary Spreadsheet as a worksheet. Gather all your financial records for the past six months. Complete a Monthly Expense Spreadsheet for each month and enter these figures on the Annual Expense Summary Spreadsheet.

Add each line to get your total for each category. Then divide by 6 to get your average per month for each category. These figures will be the best estimate of your monthly projections if you continue the way you're spending and can now be entered in the "Monthly Projections" column of your "official" spreadsheet.

Important: Be aware of any large bills you pay only once or twice a year and be sure to factor them in. (These tend to be accrual expenses.)

The Middle Management Method. *Recommended for:* people with some experience and adequate records who are not willing or able to take the time to assemble complete information.

Advantages: moderate information, moderate expenditure of time and energy.

Disadvantage: greater possibility of error due to choosing non-representative months and omitting relevant accrual data.

MANAGEMENT TIP ▟▜▼▼▼▼▼▼▼▼▼▼▼▼▼▼▼▼▼▼▼▼▼▼▙

 When formulating your projections for the current year, it's important that your expenses, including the 10 percent you pay yourself first, don't exceed 100 percent of your income. If your projections for monthly expenses are greater than 100 percent, you're programming yourself to spend more than you have available. The result? Negative cash flow and, eventually, debt.

▙▼▼▼▼▼▼▼▼▼▼▼▼▼▼▼▼▼▼▼▼▼▼▼▼▼▼▼▼▼▼▼▜

How it works: Do the very same things outlined above, only do it for three months. Modify all the computations accordingly (remember to divide by 3 instead of by 6) and be especially careful to take large accrual items into account, since some of them may not show up in a three-month period. Enter your three-month figures in the "Monthly Projections" column of your "official" spreadsheet.

The Easy Start-Up Method. Recommended for: people with inadequate records or no time right now.

Advantage: minimal expenditure of time and energy.

Disadvantage: minimal information.

How it works: Since you've probably never done a comprehensive program like this before, begin by simply tracking your expenses and entering the data as you go. For now, forget about having monthly projections to monitor your spending. You don't yet have the information you need to make these projections. However, by the end of the year, you'll have generated the information you'll need to make monthly projections for next year. So you'll be able to start off the new year with a bang! You'll begin by simply entering your monthly expenses directly onto your "official" spreadsheet.

TEN STEPS TO YEAR-END COMPLETION

At the end of the year, here's what you do to gather the critical information you'll need to close out this year's finances and launch Your Personal Money Management System for next year.

1. Add up the amount of money spent in each category for each month. These sums will go in the "Totals" column at the far right of the page.

2. Divide the sums by 12 to get an average per month for each category.

3. Log this information in the "Average per Month" column. These are the figures that'll assist you in determining your monthly projections for next year.

4. If you began keeping track of expenses somewhere in the middle of the year, figure the average per month for the months you've tracked and multiply the amount by 12. Doing this for any category will give you a good estimate of your yearly expenses for that category.

5. Add up the "Monthly Projections" column and enter the amount at the bottom of the page in the "Totals" line.

6. Add up your spending for each month and place the monthly amounts at the bottom of the page in the "Totals" line.

7. Add up the "Totals" column (at the far right of the spreadsheet) to find out how much you spent during the entire year.

8. Add up the "Average per Month" column to see how much you tended to spend each month.

9. To check the accuracy of your work, add up each month's total expenses (the "Totals" line at the bottom of the spreadsheet) and compare the figure with the sum of all the amounts in the "Totals" column (at the far right of the spreadsheet). These two amounts should be the same . . . the exact amount your family has spent for the year. If they're not, you've probably made a mathematical error and need to check your work.

10. Begin your financial planning for next year. The figures on this spreadsheet (combined with your income projections for next year) will provide you with the information you need to determine two important aspects of next year's money management program: your accrual accounts and your monthly projections.

Good news: When you complete the following Action Steps, you'll have set up more than 90 percent of your tracking system. Congratulations! You're in the homestretch now!

ACTION STEPS ∼∼∼∼∼∼∼∼∼∼∼∼∼∼∼∼∼∼∼∼∼∼∼∼∼

1. Using the information from your Monthly Expense Spreadsheet, enter your expense categories on the Annual Expense Summary Spreadsheet. Be sure to use separate lines for any categories you've combined on the monthly sheet. Include your accrual categories.

2. Using one of the methods outlined in "Setting Up Your Spreadsheet," begin entering your figures. (If you elected the third choice, this will happen as soon as you have completed your first Monthly Expense Spreadsheet.)

3. Place your completed spreadsheets in the folder labeled "Annual Income and Expense Records."

4. Congratulate yourself for your work. Few things can build self-esteem more quickly than successful actions and self-acknowledgment for those efforts.

5. Make an appointment with yourself to read chapter 15, "Step 9: Finishing the Year Right." Write down the appointment and keep it.

CHAPTER *15*

STEP 9: FINISHING THE YEAR RIGHT

If you're spending all that you earn, you might have a terrific standard of living, but you're certainly not increasing your wealth. As a matter of fact, your likelihood of ever really becoming wealthy is remote.

As we've always stressed: *How much you earn is much less important than how much of what you earn you keep.*

If you're spending more than you're earning, you're actually mortgaging your future earnings. In essence, you're creating *negative* wealth, more commonly known as *debt*.

However . . . if you're earning more than you're spending, or if you're spending less than you're earning, you're creating surplus funds to increase your wealth and realize your dreams.

That's the goal of Financial Freedom.

WHAT'S A YEAR-END WRAP-UP?

So far, you've learned how to track income and expenses. Now we'll show you how to look at them *together* so that you'll have an accurate picture of your bottom line at the end of every year.

When the year ends and your tax returns have been prepared, you'll be ready to do your Year-End Wrap-Up. Think of this process as: (1) a way to measure your success in implementing your Financial Freedom program; and (2) a way to measure how much *more* money you've added to your Wealth-Building Account.

The simple-to-use form on page 232 answers the all-important question about your financial year: *What is the relationship between your income and your expenses?*

Completing this form at year's end will show you this crucial information.

- Your annual net gain or loss
- Exactly how much you've added to your Wealth-Building Acount by paying yourself first

YEAR-END WRAP-UP: THE RICH AND GOLDIE BANKS COMPANY

For an example of how this annual process works, let's check in with our friends Rich and Goldie. You'll find their completed Year-End Wrap-Up form on the opposite page.

Let's assume it's April 10, 1994. Rich and Goldie have completed their income tax returns and mailed them in five days early. They now have all their financial figures for 1993. Here's how they've used them to complete their Year-End Wrap-Up form. For purposes of this example, we'll assume the Banks family ended the year in accordance with its estimate on the Current Cash Flow form.

1. Salary. Here they listed Rich's gross salaried income for the year—$36,000.

2. Other business. They entered the gross income from their mail-order business—$15,600.

3. Interest or dividends used as income. This refers to money received from bank accounts or investments that is used as monthly income to pay bills. In Rich and Goldie's case, this was not applicable.

THE BANKS FAMILY'S YEAR-END WRAP-UP—1993

Income

$ 36,000	1. Salary
$ 15,600	2. Other business
$ 0	3. Interest or dividends used as income
$ 0	4. Other (list)
$ 51,600	5. Total income

Expenses

$ 2,000	6. Paid to myself and my family
$ 0	7. Other savings or retirement accounts
$ 3,500	8. Federal income taxes
$ 1,500	9. State income taxes
$ 0	10. Local taxes (if applicable)
$ 1,850	11. Social Security
$ 320	12. State disability insurance
$ 42,430	13. Remaining expenses
$ 51,600	14. Total expenses
$ 51,600	15. Total income
$ 51,600	16. Total expenses
$ 0	17. Net gain/loss for the year
$ 2,000	18. Amount added to Wealth-Building Account (sum of lines 6, 7 and possibly a portion of 17)
3.88 %	19. Percentage added to Wealth-Building Account

4. Other (list). This means any other income that is used to pay monthly bills. Once again, this category was not applicable for the Banks family.

5. Total income. By adding the entries on the first four lines, Rich and Goldie arrived at their total income for the year.

6. Paid to myself and my family. This entry begins the Banks family's list of expenses. Each month, Rich and Goldie paid themselves $167, which they placed in an individual retirement account (IRA). At year's end, they had contributed $2,000.

Note: If you think it's odd to list IRA payments (as well as any other money paid to yourself) as expenses, here's the logic: Rich and Goldie paid out an average of $167 each month, which was transferred from their monthly income into their Wealth-Building Account. Even though they paid it to themselves, it's still a payment and therefore tracked as an expense. (Actually, it's the best of all possible expenses because Rich and Goldie are making an investment in themselves and their family.)

7. Other savings or retirement accounts. Rich and Goldie have no savings other than their IRA, so this line is not applicable.

8–12. Taxes and insurance. Here they listed various taxes (for which they had accurate figures), Social Security and state disability insurance.

13. Remaining expenses. This amount was easily computed by taking the total from the family's Annual Expense Summary Spreadsheet at the end of the year and subtracting any money that had been paid either to them ("Pay Yourself First") or to taxes. (These have already been taken into account above.)

14. Total expenses. When Rich and Goldie added up the ex-

MANAGEMENT TIP ▼▼▼▼▼▼▼▼▼▼▼▼▼▼▼▼▼▼▼▼▼▼▼▼▼

Consider saving your Year-End Wrap-Up sheets in a special file folder. We do. As a matter of fact, we have more than a decade's worth of these records. They let us see at a glance exactly which aspects of our finances tend to change from year to year and by exactly how much.

▼▼▼▼▼▼▼▼▼▼▼▼▼▼▼▼▼▼▼▼▼▼▼▼▼▼▼▼▼▼▼

penses shown on lines 6 through 13, they saw that their annual expenses were $51,600.

15. Total income *and* 16. Total expenses. These figures are simply the amounts listed in lines 5 and 14, transferred down the page to make the next computation easier.

17. Net gain/loss for the year. This amount is figured by subtracting total expenses (line 16) from total income (line 15). This form shows us that the Banks family had a net gain of $0 for 1993.

18. Amount added to Wealth-Building Account. This very important figure is determined by adding lines 6 and 7.

19. Percentage of income added to Wealth-Building Account. We define *Financial Freedom* as increasing your wealth by at least 10 percent of your income each year. To determine how their family compared with our recommendation, Rich and Goldie added their net gain (line 17) to the amount added to Wealth-Building Account (line 18) and divided the sum by their total income (line 15). As you see, they increased their wealth in 1993 by 3.88 percent of their income. This information let Rich and Goldie know that they have some work to do if they're to upgrade their standard of saving to a level that's financially healthy.

ACTION STEPS ~~~~~~~~~~~~~~~~~~~~~~~~~~~~~~~

1. Complete your Year-End Wrap-Up sheet now, penciling in your "best guesstimate" of what you think the accurate figures will be on December 31. You'll find the blank form on page 232.

2. When the end of the year rolls around—and you have your real annual figures—see how accurate your projections turn out to be. Complete the sheet with your annual figures.

3. Get a new file folder and label it "Year-End Wrap-Up." Place your Year-End Wrap-Up forms in the folder.

4. Acknowledge and appreciate yourself. You're rapidly approaching the finish line of Your Personal Money Management System.

5. Make an appointment to read chapter 16, "Step 10: Keeping Score Every Month." Write down the appointment and keep it.

CHAPTER
16

STEP 10: KEEPING
SCORE EVERY MONTH

Does any of the following sound all too familiar?

"How in the world did I spend all that money so fast?"

"You mean I'm overdrawn on my checking account again?"

"But I just got *out* of debt."

"Help! A black hole in space is eating all my money!"

Keeping Score to the rescue!

What's "Keeping Score"? It's an important step because it allows you to monitor the relationship between income and expenses each month.

By tracking and reviewing what's happening from month to month with both income and expenses, you can easily see whether you're on or off course *as you go along rather than after the fact at the end of the year*. It's especially helpful for people whose income varies.

All the information you'll need to monitor your

monthly financial picture is already recorded on your

Annual Income Summary Spreadsheet. Look it over and read about how Rich and Goldie use Keeping Score to successfully monitor their money.

To show you how this works, let's look at the financial records of the Banks family.

KEEPING SCORE: THE RICH AND GOLDIE BANKS COMPANY

On page 156, you'll find the Banks Family's Annual Income Summary Spreadsheet for January through June 1993. You can use this example as a reference while completing your own form. The only difference between this form and the earlier one from step 6 is that the "Keeping Score" section at the bottom of the page has now been filled in with financial data.

Let's take a closer look at this information and how to gather it to complete the "Keeping Score" part of the form.

1. Enter the amount of your monthly income. Check the Banks family's spreadsheet, and you'll see, for example, that the amount entered for January is $4,300. Where did Rich and Goldie get this information? Simple. This figure comes directly from the total monthly income they tabulated at the top of the form for January.

2. Enter your deductions for the month. If you're salaried, these deductions are itemized on your paycheck stub. If you're self-employed, check your quarterly estimated state and federal tax payments. In January, the Banks family's deductions were $600.

3. Compute your net income per month by subtracting your deductions from your monthly income. Rich and Goldie's net income in January: $3,700.

4. Enter your personal expenses for the month. You can get this information from either your Monthly Expense Spreadsheet or your Annual Expense Summary Spreadsheet. The Banks family's living expenses for January: $3,403.

5. Enter your business expenses for the month, if relevant. Since Rich and Goldie have a sideline mail-order business, they have monthly business expenses. In January: $278.

6. Compute your monthly net by subtracting your personal and business expenses from your net income. For example, for January, Rich and Goldie's monthly net was:

$3,700 − 3,403 − 278 = $19

THE BANKS FAMILY'S ANNUAL						
1993 YEAR	MONTHLY PRO-JECTIONS	JAN.	FEB.	MAR.	APR.	MAY
1	MONTHLY INCOME					
2	Gross Salary	3,000	3,000	3,000	3,000	3,000	3,000
3	Mail-Order	1,100	1,300	1,000	1,500	1,400	1,300
4	Other (specify)	0	0	0	0	0	0
5							
6	Totals	4,100	4,300	4,000	4,500	4,400	4,300
7							
8							
9	ASSET INCOME						
10	CD Interest	190	160	165	163	166	169
11	Other Interest	50	49	52	51	52	53
12	Gifts	0	0	0	0	0	0
13	Paid to Myself	167	167	167	167	167	167
14							
15	Totals	407	376	384	381	385	389
16							
17							
18	KEEPING SCORE						
19	Monthly Income		4,300	4,000	4,500	4,400	4,300
20	Deductions		600	600	600	600	600
21	Net Income		3,700	3,400	3,900	3,800	3,700
22	Personal Expenses		3,403	3,260	3,105	3,100	3,199
23	Business Expenses		278	250	360	330	310
24	Monthly Net		+19	−110	+435	+370	+191
25	Cumulative		+19	−91	+344	+714	+905
26							
27							
28							
29							
30							

This was logged on the spreadsheet as "+19" because the amount for January was a surplus.

7. Finally, by adding or subtracting your monthly net as you go along from month to month, you easily see your cumulative net, or how you're doing as the year unfolds.

	INCOME SUMMARY SPREADSHEET								
JUNE	JULY	AUG.	SEPT.	OCT.	NOV.	DEC.	TOTALS	AVERAGE PER MONTH	
									1
3,000							18,000	3,000	2
1,300							7,800	1,300	3
0							0	0	4
									5
4,300							25,800	4,300	6
									7
									8
									9
173							996	166	10
55							312	52	11
600							600	100	12
167							1,002	167	13
									14
995							2,910	485	15
									16
									17
									18
4,300									19
600									20
3,700									21
3,038									22
315									23
+347									24
+1,252									25
									26
									27
									28
									29
									30

SPOTTING EARLY WARNING SIGNALS

As you track from month to month, you'll see if and when you're heading off course so that you can immediately take whatever actions are needed to bring you back on course again.

For example, if high expenses are resulting in negative cash flow, you can decide to put more energy into increasing your income. Or you can choose to reduce your spending to bring it in line with your income.

On the other hand, you could happily find that your income is greater than you projected. That gives you room to increase your spending in whatever area you choose: a new coat or a deposit in your dream vacation account. Even better, you may decide to pay yourself *more than the usual!* Your possibilities are endless.

ACTION STEPS ~~~~~~~~~~~~~~~~~~~~

1. Get your Annual Income Summary Spreadsheet from its folder and complete the "Keeping Score" section.

2. When you're done, return the sheet to its folder.

3. Take a deep breath. You're only steps away from the finish line of Your Personal Money Management System.

4. Make an appointment with yourself to read chapter 17, "Step 11: Keeping Track of Your Personal Fortune," where you'll break the tape and cross the finish line.

CHAPTER *17*

STEP 11: KEEPING TRACK OF YOUR PERSONAL FORTUNE

In many ways, the Assets Tracking Form will provide you with the most important information of all.

Its purpose is to track your wealth-building assets from year to year. In essence, this form will show you at a glance the bottom line on your personal wealth. (Talk about important information!)

ASSETS TRACKING: THE RICH AND GOLDIE BANKS COMPANY

Once again, let's look to the Banks family for an example of how to fill out our form. The Banks Family's Assets Tracking Form is on page 160.

As you can see, this form is simple and straightforward. (Isn't that a relief?) It easily displays five categories of information.

Date. This is simply the date that you filled in the current information. For Rich and Goldie, that's July 10,

THE BANKS FAMILY'S ASSETS TRACKING FORM

JULY 10, 1993

Asset	Current Value	Year-End Value
Bank of Wealth CD	$27,100	
Home equity	$23,000	
Mail-order business	$36,000	
Cash on hand	$380	
Auto #1 (3 years old)	$7,000	
Auto #2 (5 years old)	$4,700	
Peace of Mind insurance policy (cash surrender value)	$2,800	
Checking account #1	$3,341	
Checking account #2	$2,735	
Global Growth Fund (mutual fund)	$4,208	
Pacific Rim Fund (mutual fund)	$4,792	
3 favorite artist lithographs	$2,700	
Garnet and pearl necklace	$1,900	
Wedding rings	$1,700	
Gold coins—2 maple leaf	$750	
IRA	$12,400	
Totals	$135,506	

1993. As you continue gathering this information year after year, the date is a handy way to organize the progress of your financial assets.

Asset. Here each of your assets is itemized for easy viewing. Rich and Goldie listed 16 assets, ranging from a certificate of deposit (CD) to automobiles to jewelry.

Current value. The monetary value of each asset is displayed under the heading "Current Value." For example, the Banks family's home equity was valued at $23,000.

Year-end value. As you see, this column is blank. But as 1993 came to a close, Rich and Goldie will have sat down and reappraised each item listed in their "Assets" column. These new figures would then have been logged on the form.

Totals. When completed, this form will display two different totals, conveniently placed side-by-side for comparison. The first is the total current value of your assets. The second is the total year-end value of your assets. By looking at these figures at year's end, you'll see the growth of your personal wealth. So far, Rich and Goldie had entered the total value of their assets as of July 10, 1993: $135,506.

Now It's Your Turn!

If your head is still spinning from your last interlude with a spreadsheet, take heart! Almost *nothing* will be easier than filling

MENTAL TIP ▰▼▼▼▼▼▼▼▼▼▼▼▼▼▼▼▼▼▼▼▼▼▼▼▼▼▼▼▼▼▰

Remember, psychologically it's vitally important to positively reinforce your successes—in this case, your completion of the process of launching Your Personal Money Management System. By positively reinforcing this achievement, you continue to program your Private Access Learning System (PALS) to set you up for your next success. What's a special reward you could give yourself as soon as you complete this form? Dinner out? A night at the movies? A new sweater? A candlelit bath? Whatever it is . . . just go and do it!

▲▼▲▼▲▼▲▼▲▼▲▼▲▼▲▼▲▼▲▼▲▼▲▼▲▼▲▼▲▼▲▼▲▼▲▼▲

out your Assets Tracking Form. Honest. Just look how easy it was for Rich and Goldie. Your blank form can be found on page 233.

To begin, simply pull out your completed Current Assets form. Then transfer the information onto this new form, placing the data in the appropriate places. Voilà! You don't have to touch this form again until December 31. When the current year comes to an end, you enter the year-end values of your assets.

Now here's some really good news: Once this form is completed, you'll have taken a monumental step toward managing the growth of your personal fortune. Why? Because 100 percent of Your Personal Money Management System is now in place. And you're ready to handle all that wealth you're about to create!

ACTION STEPS ~~~~~~~~~~~~~~~~~~~~~~~~~~~

1. Complete your Assets Tracking Form by listing your assets. Here you can be more specific than you were when you first viewed your assets in chapter 8, "Step 2: Getting a Handle on Your Current Assets."

2. Reward yourself. *You deserve it!*

Part
III

"Man was born to be rich or inevitably to grow rich through the use of his faculties."

—RALPH WALDO EMERSON

THINK WEALTHY,
FEEL WEALTHY, BE WEALTHY

CHAPTER *18*

CREATING WEALTH

You don't have to understand the entire theory of electricity to turn on a light switch. And you don't need to know everything about *creativity* to create wealth. (And lots of it!)

In this chapter, we'll be giving you a *working* knowledge of the creative process: how to change the light bulb when your creativity burns out, what to do when you blow a creative fuse and how to locate the right switch to turn on the right idea.

Want proof that you can create without knowing anything formal about the process? Just look at your life right now. You're creating something every minute of the day. Whatever is happening now in your life, you had a hand in creating it.

The challenge is not so much being creative but handling what we call competing creativity.

What is "competing creativity"?

Picture the creative process as a train on a track from New York City to Chicago. The engineer driving the train doesn't have to consciously focus on "Chicago, Chicago, Chicago..." every second of the trip. The track does that for her. All she has to do is make sure **167** the train goes at the proper speed and halts at all scheduled stops.

Wouldn't it be great if creativity were like that train, chugging without hesitation to its destination? In fact, creativity is more like a truck barreling down a highway. A truck driver hauling cargo from New York City to Chicago can begin to doubt whether he really wants to go to Chicago. Somewhere west of Pittsburgh, he might decide to go to Georgia instead. After all, there is no track to hold him on course to Chicago.

So the driver makes a left turn and begins traveling south. What about Chicago, the original destination? Forget it, we're going to Atlanta for dinner. But on the way to Atlanta, the driver all of a sudden realizes the cargo is perishable and needs to be delivered in Chicago by a specific time. Whoops, let's make a U-turn and get back on the road to Chicago. That truck driver just had a run-in with competing creativity.

Many people operate their creative process much like that truck driver. Every time you change your mind about your destination or goals, the energy you've established along the line to Chicago gets interrupted, and you have to begin all over, establishing a new line of creative energy.

If Michelangelo had painted the ceiling of the Sistine Chapel the way many people paint their lives, he probably would still be painting today, and the job would be about half done.

What supports you in successfully achieving your goals and fulfilling your dreams is learning how to lay down a type of inner track that runs from New York City to Chicago so that no matter how often you forget your destination, the track will keep you on course and moving in the direction of your goals. We refer to the laying down of the track as "having a clear picture" of where you want to be and the moving along the track as "implementing your Financial Freedom program."

As it turns out, the Financial Freedom process is an express train from the New York City of where you are now financially to the Chicago of where you'd like to be. But first of all, you need to lay the *track!*

GIVE YOURSELF PERMISSION TO DREAM

Dreams help lay that track by giving clues about where you want to be. But in our private counseling sessions and our public group seminars, we've found that a surprising number of people are *afraid* to dream of being wealthy. Because they've experienced disappointment associated with unfulfilled dreams in the past—often when they were very young—they're unwilling to risk dreaming again, lest they experience hurt again.

Sometimes it can be quite challenging to assist people in consciously opening up to their dreams. But without those dreams, you condemn yourself to a life of unconsciously driving from New York City to an unknown destination and never arriving anyplace you can recognize as a goal. Why? Because you haven't taken sufficient time to clearly establish a destination.

In our seminars, we include a process that dramatically brings home the importance of a clear picture in going toward your goal. We divide people into small groups of six to eight and have them sit in circles. Then we put a fairly easy jigsaw puzzle in the center of each group and tell them to complete the puzzle in the shortest amount of time. When each group is done, they raise their hands, and we record the time it took each group to complete the puzzle.

What participants don't know is that we've actually set up three different situations. In the first situation, the picture on the box lid matches the picture on the puzzle. In the second situation, the picture on the box is different from the picture on the puzzle. In the third situation, there's no picture at all on the box—it's blank.

The results are almost invariably the same. The groups with the matching picture and puzzle finish in the shortest time; the groups with no picture take the longest. The middle groups, the ones with the mismatched picture and puzzle, finish sooner than the no-picture groups. Conclusion? *The clearer the picture, the more efficient you are at successfully achieving your goal. Even an inaccurate picture is better than no picture at all.*

Why? The clearer the picture, the more powerful the message to your Private Access Learning System (PALS).

INTENTION VERSUS METHOD

Some people are unwilling to dream because they fear disapproval. Others don't dream because they're anxious about how to go about achieving those goals. That's like not turning on the light switch because you're uncertain how the electricity will get to the bulb.

Don't worry. Creativity often thrives on uncertainty. You don't have to be concerned *at all* about how you'll achieve your goals when you're in the process of identifying them. Don't be even slightly concerned about the methods you'll use. Just be steadfast in your determination to reach your goals. We call this "holding a clear intention."

Remember: At this stage, all you're doing is laying down the track to greater wealth. It's not necessary to know what you're going to drive down that track, how long it's going to take to get there and what you'll do along the way. The only thing you have to be clear about now is where you want to go and the strength of your intention to get there.

In the chapters that immediately follow, we'll work with you to lay down the track you'll use to guide yourself toward increased wealth. Then we'll share with you some of the most powerful techniques we know for moving yourself along the track you've established.

ACTION STEPS ⌇⌇⌇⌇⌇⌇⌇⌇⌇⌇⌇⌇⌇⌇⌇⌇⌇⌇⌇⌇⌇

1. Assume that you've just won a major sweepstakes. You've been notified that Ed McMahon will personally be handing you a check for $10 million. What will you do with all that money? Get a sheet of paper and begin listing all the ways you anticipate using your newfound wealth. In particular, pay careful attention to the things you plan on doing after you buy the new house, the new car, the new clothes and so on. These often hold clues to some of the deeper aspirations you'd like to realize in your life.

2. Start a file folder called "Ideal Scenes and Already There Reports." We'll explain both of these methods to you in the next few chapters. For now, you can place your list of how you'd use your $10 million in the folder.

3. Make an appointment with yourself to read chapter 19, "Imagining Your Ideal Scenes." Keep that appointment with yourself.

4. Congratulate yourself! You're opening the floodgates of your very own powerful creative flow.

CHAPTER *19*

IMAGINING YOUR
IDEAL SCENES

We trust you had a splendid time figuring out all the ways to use your $10 million. Notice we didn't ask you to list the ways you plan on *spending* your newfound money. Rather, we asked you what you'd *do* with it and how you'd *use* it.

As we mentioned earlier, there's a strong connection between being able to attract money to you *and* having a purpose that attracts it. The stronger your purpose, the more likely you are to be successful and wealthy.

The $10 million exercise was designed to help you recognize the *real* reasons you'd like to be wealthy—the ones that show up *after* the new house, the new car, the new clothes. Make sure you dig down deep until you understand the *real* purposes of money in your life. These hidden purposes tend to be accurate indicators of what's truly important to you. They reveal that part in you that would really like to be of service and leave this **171** world a little better than you found it. Good examples are the magnificent endowments of Bill Cosby to Spelman College and Walter Annenberg's founding of the multi-million-dollar, state-of-the-art Annenberg School of Communications at the University of Pennsylvania.

When you're in touch with a vision of where you'd like your life to go, you'll have a better understanding of your broad, fundamental goals. That will be the engine that powers your quest for creating wealth and financial well-being.

But it's time to get specific. You need a more detailed picture of where you'd like to be financially in a year or so. We have an amazing technique, the method of Ideal Scenes, that uses the gift of fantasy to help you get a very precise picture of what you'd like your assets to look like in the near future.

What's an Ideal Scene?

It's really nothing more than a clear picture of how you'd like things to be in the future.

How do you create an Ideal Scene?

Simple. You use your imagination. You make it up.

Based on our financial counseling with thousands of people, we're well aware that right now you are probably screaming "That's daydreaming—a bunch of kid's stuff!" or "Fantasies! You gotta be kidding me! I'm looking for the cold, hard facts about money."

Before you throw this book across the room, check out what Albert Einstein (no slack in the brains department) had to say about the power of fantasy: "When I examine myself and my methods of thought, I come to the conclusion that the gift of fantasy meant more to me than my talent for absorbing positive knowledge."

Good ol' Albert knew the power of his creative imagination and the importance it played in his life.

So if Einstein used it, won't you at least give it a chance?

In our own experience, as well as in our experience with people we counsel, we've found that the best time frame for most Ideal Scenes is *one year*. You can easily picture yourself one year in the future. But if you go much beyond a year, especially in these fast-moving and uncertain times, it becomes increasingly challenging for your mind to reasonably believe what you're visualizing. There are simply too many possibilities and uncertainties. In addition, most people keep financial score on a yearly basis, so looking one year into the future is practical.

GUIDELINES FOR EFFECTIVE IDEAL SCENES

If you plan on starting your Financial Freedom program some-time during the middle of the year, you may decide to develop an Ideal Scene that simply brings you to the end of the current year.

The Banks family—introduced in Part II—did just that. Rich and Goldie decided to begin their Financial Freedom program in July 1993, so they developed their Ideal Scenes to run for six months, until January 1, 1994.

Before you look at the Ideal Scenes for the Banks family—and then do your own—here are five guidelines for creating successful Ideal Scenes. Use these guidelines, and you'll be far more likely to achieve your financial goals.

1. The "At Least 50 Percent Believable" Guideline. If you de-velop an Ideal Scene for your finances and you currently have a net worth of $20,000, you're much more likely to believe an Ideal Scene that has your assets increasing to $30,000 a year from now as compared with one that has them increasing to $300,000. Not that an increase in assets from $20,000 to $300,000 in one year is impossible—it's just not very likely for most people. And an in-crease in assets to $3 million is even less believable.

An Ideal Scene that isn't believable won't support you *or* your wealth-building goals. Instead, concentrate on the everyday, nuts-and-bolts aspects of your Ideal Scenes. Make them at least 50 per-cent believable to you. Your creativity depends on your ability to get behind your dream—to see it as not only possible but *believable* as well.

2. The "Highest Good of All Concerned" Guideline. When you create and implement a new vision for your life, you are, by defini-tion, moving from the known to the unknown.

Have you ever considered the possibility that creating $10 mil-lion might not be in your best interests? We know some very wealthy people who are terribly burdened by their money and long for a simpler life.

Recently we met a man who had considerable wealth—at least $10 million. However, he's neither happy nor fulfilled. In fact, he appeared to us quite heavy-hearted at the prospect that not even one of his dreams would ever come true. For instance, when we discussed a philanthropic project he favored that had fallen apart due to infighting, his discouraged comment was "Oh well, another dream that will never happen."

How can you know beforehand whether what you're creating is going to turn out to be a benefit to your life and the lives of those around you or an albatross around your neck?

For that reason, at the bottom of every Ideal Scene we write the words "This or something better for the highest good of all concerned." This statement recognizes the "dilemma" of creation and puts our creative side on notice that this Ideal Scene is our *current best attempt* at a clear picture of what we'd like to have in our life. If our creative self is aware of a better plan, we're all for it.

3. The "Outcomes Not Actions" Guideline. When an architect begins to develop a design for a building, she meets first with the individual or team in charge of the entire project to get a first impression of the kind of building they have in mind and its purpose. Next she goes to the building site to discuss how the project can be accomplished at that location. The architect then spends considerable time in her office conceiving and drawing different designs to be submitted to the owners for approval.

Up to this point, no one has given much thought to how the building will actually be constructed or when it will be completed. And that's as it should be. The design phase of a project reflects the architect's vision of a building that can be created.

In exactly the same way, Ideal Scenes are a way for you, the architect of your finances, to design a financial reality that can be created. You are looking at the *outcome* you'd like. You're not looking for specific action steps you'll need to take to get you there. In fact, we know people who've actually sabotaged their dreams by abandoning them because they couldn't see how they'd possibly accomplish them. *It's important for you to trust the creative process!* By identifying outcomes and establishing a clear intention, the methods needed to realize those outcomes will become apparent.

4. The "Floors Not Ceilings" Guideline. Remember the "At Least 50 Percent Believable" guideline? We told you to keep your financial dreams believable—to envision going from $20,000 to

$30,000, not from $20,000 to $300,000. At the same time, though, we don't want you to *exclude* the possibility of something marvelously unexpected happening next year that would skyrocket your assets to $300,000.

Believe it or not, there's a very simple way to build your Ideal Scenes so that they are at least 50 percent believable *and* have unlimited potential. For each figure in your Ideal Scenes, follow it with the words "or more." For example, say you have an investment currently valued at $15,000. It's at least 50 percent believable to you that next year at this time your investment could be worth $18,000. That represents a healthy 20 percent increase, and you'd really prefer to see it go much higher. On the portion of your Ideal Scene showing that investment, you'd write "$18,000 or more." This sets $18,000 in your creative consciousness as a floor, while the "or more" allows for the possibility of a larger increase. No restrictions, constrictions or ceilings allowed!

5. The "Anticipate a Miracle" Guideline. Oral Roberts is the man credited with making famous the phrase "Expect a miracle." And while we agree that he was on the right track, when it comes to creating wealth it's important to be very careful and explicit with the words we use. When we "expect" something, there's a sense that it's actually coming—and coming soon. We're already looking forward to it. This can easily set up an attachment to a particular outcome, leading to disappointment if what's expected doesn't materialize.

On the other hand, when you "anticipate" something, you neutrally examine your goal in your mind's eye *without* the emotional energy of attachment to an outcome that's associated with expectation. It's a subtle but important distinction to make. And to make it, you must understand and practice the skill of "neutral active participation."

We use it when planning our vacation each year. We get an idea of a place we'd like to visit and immediately begin researching the area. (We probably research ten places a year.) We contact travel agents, send for brochures, call hotels for literature and make lists of activities available and places to visit. We become very actively involved in the process, "anticipating" or preparing for the possibility that we might go there. We enjoy gathering the information but don't have any attachments to or expectations about the places we're considering. It's only after we've completed our research, carefully reviewed our options and actually made reservations that anticipation begins to turn into expectancy.

In terms of finances, it's important to free yourself from the mental attachment and related emotional reaction of disappointment that go with expectation. When doing an Ideal Scene, dare to anticipate a miracle—like winning the lottery, doubling your salary, inheriting a bundle—but don't be disappointed if one doesn't show up.

IDEAL SCENE FOR ASSETS: THE RICH AND GOLDIE BANKS COMPANY

So taking these five guidelines into consideration, let's look at the Banks Family's Ideal Scene for Assets. On page 88, you'll find the Banks Family's Current Assets form, and on the opposite page, Rich and Goldie's clear picture of their desired assets. Let's look at this Ideal Scene together, starting in the upper right with the certificate of deposit and going clockwise.

Certificate of deposit (CD). As of July 10, 1993, it was worth $27,100. By January 1, 1994, given interest rates, it could easily have been worth at least an additional $1,200, for a total of $28,300 or more. However, Rich and Goldie might not renew it when it comes due, since they've learned about other investment strategies that can potentially yield a better return.

Home equity. The equity in the Banks family's home could have increased from $23,000 to $28,000 or more. The family lives in a good area where real estate values are increasing slightly. In addition, over the course of the last six months of 1993, Rich and Goldie will have paid off some of the principal on their mortgage.

Business. Their mail-order business is small and has some cash value. Both Rich and Goldie had been working to increase sales and could visualize its value of $36,000 easily increasing to $40,000 or more.

Cash on hand. Rich and Goldie planned on increasing their cash on hand from $380 to $600 or more.

Automobiles. The family autos will have done most of their depreciating, and Rich and Goldie will have paid off a significant

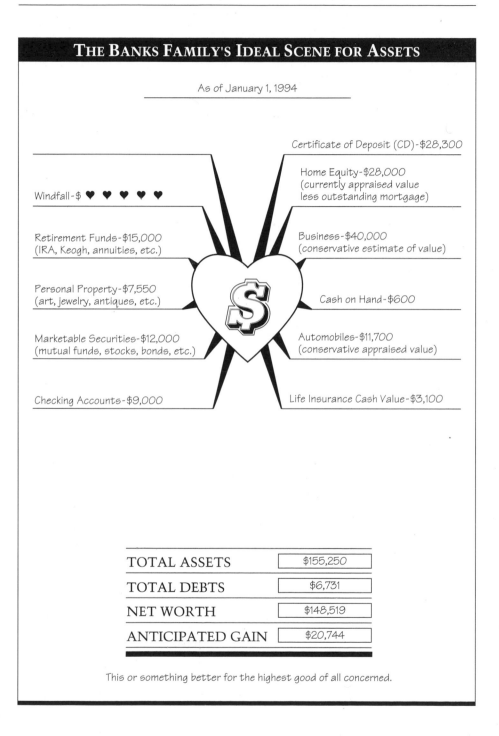

THE BANKS FAMILY'S IDEAL SCENE FOR ASSETS

As of January 1, 1994

Certificate of Deposit (CD)-$28,300

Home Equity-$28,000
(currently appraised value
less outstanding mortgage)

Windfall-$ ♥ ♥ ♥ ♥ ♥

Retirement Funds-$15,000
(IRA, Keogh, annuities, etc.)

Business-$40,000
(conservative estimate of value)

Personal Property-$7,550
(art, jewelry, antiques, etc.)

Cash on Hand-$600

Marketable Securities-$12,000
(mutual funds, stocks, bonds, etc.)

Automobiles-$11,700
(conservative appraised value)

Checking Accounts-$9,000

Life Insurance Cash Value-$3,100

TOTAL ASSETS	$155,250
TOTAL DEBTS	$6,731
NET WORTH	$148,519
ANTICIPATED GAIN	$20,744

This or something better for the highest good of all concerned.

amount of their outstanding auto loans, so the value of their autos remains at $11,700.

Life insurance cash value. The cash surrender value of their life insurance policy, placed at $2,800, will have increased slightly, so they estimated it at $3,100 or more. Also, they're investigating cashing in the policy and replacing it with term insurance—which costs less for equal coverage.

Checking accounts. Rich and Goldie planned on increasing the amount in their checking accounts because they recognized the need for a greater level of cash reserves. They'll have put some of the 10 percent they pay themselves into their Wealth-Building Account, so an increase from $6,076 to $9,000 or more is likely.

Marketable securities. Rich and Goldie wanted to see their securities increase substantially. These investments were worth $9,000, and Rich and Goldie would have liked them valued at $12,000 or more by January 1, 1994. Since some of their holdings are invested in companies with potential, it's believable to visualize that level of increase.

Personal property. Rich and Goldie planned on buying a small painting, and their lithographs will probably have been worth more in six months. An increase from $7,050 to $7,550 or more is certainly at least 50 percent believable.

Retirement funds. Rich and Goldie planned on putting $2,000 into their individual retirement account (IRA). Since that money is tax-deferred income, their $12,400 could easily have been valued at $15,000 or more by the beginning of 1994.

Important note: Rich and Goldie eliminated one category from their Ideal Scene—"Money Owed to You." Since they're not in the habit of loaning money, they decided to replace it with another category: "Windfall." It's one of our favorite categories and one that too few people know about. Essentially, the "Windfall" category is a space set aside for luck, chance and wishful thinking. We'll tell you more about how to maximize this opportunity later.

Did we detect a slight flinch at the mention of wishful thinking?

Well, what's wrong with wishful thinking? Not a thing . . . if you approach it the right way. Anticipate a miracle, but don't *expect* a miracle. It's energizing to visualize yourself winning the lottery or the sweepstakes, and it can be inspiring to fantasize what you'll do with your windfall. What's *not* smart is *counting* on a windfall to pay your bills, get you out of debt or secure your future financially.

In other words, go ahead and have fun making Ideal Scenes for a new house, a new car, a terrific vacation or a life of philanthropic endeavors. Having these types of "positive fantasies" on your Ideal Scenes sends a clear message to yourself that you're *open* to receiving greater abundance.

This is why you see the string of hearts on the "Windfall" line of the Banks Family's Ideal Scene for Assets—and no dollar values. In this category, the sky's the limit, and if nothing monetary comes of it, you at least had fun while imagining the possibilities and mentally preparing yourself for greater prosperity.

The bottom line. Now take a look at the Banks family's bottom line. Total assets have jumped from $135,506 to $155,250, a gain of $19,744 for this family in only six months. Assuming Rich and Goldie will also have reduced their debt by about $1,000 (by paying off their credit cards each month and by paying off the principal on their auto payments), their net worth would have gone from $127,775 to $148,519, a net increase of $20,744. If they can keep up this rate for ten years, their net worth would easily climb to well over $300,000.

This gain of $20,744 is their Ideal Scene for what they would have liked their assets to be in six months. It's a specific picture reflecting their financial goals for their assets as of January 1, 1994. If you're starting your Financial Freedom program later in the year, it might make sense for you to visualize a year and a few months into the future. For example, if you are beginning in September or October 1994, you could do your Ideal Scene for January 1, 1996, since January 1, 1995, is but a few months away and doesn't give you much time to implement the creative process.

IDEAL SCENE FOR CASH FLOW:
THE RICH AND GOLDIE BANKS COMPANY

Now that you're familiar with the process for developing Ideal Scenes, let's take a look at the Banks Family's Ideal Scene for Cash Flow. On page 104, you'll find the Banks Family's Cash Flow form, and on page 180, a clear picture of their desired cash flow. Let's

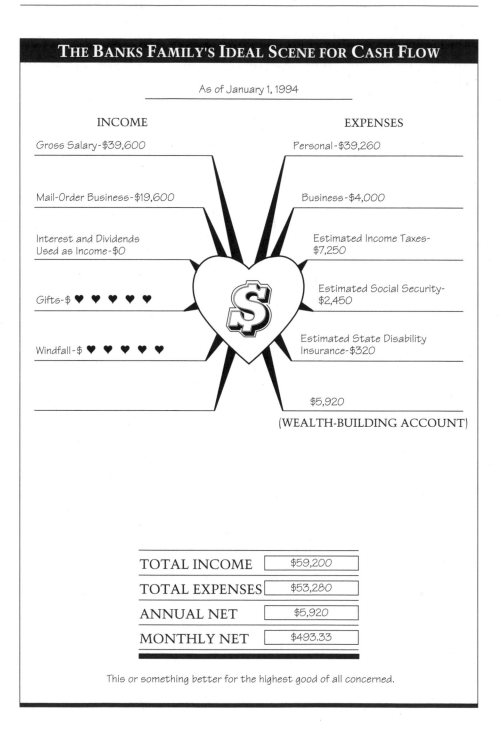

THE BANKS FAMILY'S IDEAL SCENE FOR CASH FLOW

As of January 1, 1994

INCOME

Gross Salary-$39,600

Mail-Order Business-$19,600

Interest and Dividends
Used as Income-$0

Gifts-$ ♥ ♥ ♥ ♥ ♥

Windfall-$ ♥ ♥ ♥ ♥ ♥

EXPENSES

Personal-$39,260

Business-$4,000

Estimated Income Taxes-
$7,250

Estimated Social Security-
$2,450

Estimated State Disability
Insurance-$320

$5,920

(WEALTH-BUILDING ACCOUNT)

TOTAL INCOME	$59,200
TOTAL EXPENSES	$53,280
ANNUAL NET	$5,920
MONTHLY NET	$493.33

This or something better for the highest good of all concerned.

look at this Ideal Scene together, starting on the left with the "Income" side of the form.

Salary. Rich had been at his job for several years, had received positive performance evaluations and felt he was due for a raise. So he built in a 10 percent, or $3,600, pay increase, which would have brought his gross salary from $36,000 to $39,600 a year.

Mail-order business. Since Rich and Goldie had been putting more effort into it—implementing much of what they learned in a seminar on direct mail marketing—the business had been growing. They found it quite believable to anticipate an increase of at least $4,000, from $15,600 to $19,600 or more.

Interest and dividends used as income. Rich and Goldie wanted all their interest and dividends to continue to go toward building their assets. They didn't intend to use any of their interest as income to pay expenses, so this area is again $0.

Gifts. While Rich and Goldie didn't expect any gifts to speak of, the "Anticipate a Miracle" guideline reminded them to be open to an unexpected one, so they placed a string of hearts on this line.

Windfall. Again, since windfalls are rarely expected, the "Anticipate a Miracle" guideline suggests Rich and Goldie be open to receive, so they filled in this line with hearts, too.

By adding Rich's anticipated salary of $39,600 to the projected income of $19,600 or more from the mail-order business, the total expected income for the Banks family was $59,200 or more. This figure was entered into the "Total Income" box at the bottom of the Ideal Scene for Cash Flow form.

Now let's see what the "Expenses" side of the picture looks like. Placing well-thought-out figures on these lines is an *extremely* important aspect of your creative process, because these figures will serve as the major guideline for developing your expense categories for the coming year. In other words, these are the raw materials you'll use to create future wealth. We'll go step-by-step here as we show you how Rich and Goldie calculated these figures.

In a sense, developing expense goals requires what we call reverse reasoning. We begin with the balance we want to end with and work backward. It's similar to sculpting a statue. A sculptor usually envisions the already completed figure in the block of marble and simply chips away everything else. In the same way, you can derive your *expenses* by taking away everything else. We'll show you how. Ready?

Wealth-Building Account. Since Rich and Goldie committed to the Financial Freedom approach of always increasing their wealth by at least 10 percent of their total income, they planned on adding a total of $5,920 or more to their Wealth-Building Account, including the $2,000 they expected to contribute to their IRA. They arrived at this figure by taking 10 percent of their anticipated total income (in the box at the bottom of the form). They considered this a priority, because paying themselves first is the most important aspect of their wealth-building program. At the end of 1994, when all is said and done and all their bills have been paid, they plan on having increased their wealth by this amount or more. So $5,920 was also placed in the box called "Annual Net" at the bottom of the form.

Next, by subtracting $5,920 (annual net) from $59,200 (total income), Rich and Goldie saw that they could anticipate having $53,280 to use in 1994 for all the rest of their expenses. This amount was placed in the box called "Total Expenses" at the bottom of the form.

Before we continue figuring out the remaining expenses, there's one additional guideline that must be added to the five already discussed for Ideal Scenes in general. It is for use with expenses only and is a variation of the "Floors Not Ceilings" guideline. We call it the "Ceilings Not Floors" guideline, and here's how it works. You'll remember that when we're working on the aspects of our finances that we wish to *increase*, we always talk about floors but not ceilings. That's why we think "this amount or more." However, when we're looking at expenses, we want to get those to go *down* as much as possible. So in this instance, we talk about ceilings but not floors and think "this amount or less."

Let's take a look at Rich and Goldie's planning for their 1994 expenses. You can easily see how the "Ceilings Not Floors" guideline comes into play.

Business. Rich and Goldie figured these expenses next, since this is wealth-generating money that earns them income from their mail-order business. They expected to spend $3,600 by the end of 1993, and by the end of 1994 they anticipated spending a bit more, but not more than $4,000—in other words, $4,000 or less.

Taxes. Taxes must be paid sooner or later. The best approach is to pay them sooner, so you avoid the penalties, stress and hassle often associated with dealing with the Internal Revenue Service. As we see it, a little strategic planning now regarding payment of taxes is probably one of the wisest investments you'll ever make from the point of view of your psychological well-being.

The anticipated increase in income would result in an increase in taxes, and the Banks family's accountant projected that the amounts for taxes, Social Security and state disability insurance would not be more than $7,250, $2,450 and $320, respectively.

Personal expenses. Now Rich and Goldie were ready to complete the last item under "Expenses," because it's determined by all the other figures on the right side of the form. First they added the amounts already entered under "Expenses."

	$ 5,920	Wealth-Building Account
	$ 4,000	Business
	$ 7,250	Estimated income taxes
	$ 2,450	Estimated Social Security
+	$ 320	Estimated state disability insurance
=	$19,940	Total

Then they subtracted that total from the figure in the "Total Income" box. This left $39,260, which they entered on the form on the line for personal expenses. In other words, after first paying themselves 10 percent and then subtracting what they anticipated needing for business expenses, taxes, Social Security and state disability insurance, Rich and Goldie planned on having $39,260 to spend on everyday expenses.

Let's put this in perspective. The Ideal Scene for Cash Flow that Rich and Goldie intended to adopt is the plan they thought would accomplish their financial goals. It assumes certain increases in income using the guidelines for Ideal Scenes. It also provides for their increasing their wealth by $5,920 or more, paying all their bills on time and paying down their debt by $1,000. At the same time, they won't create any new debt. And they'll pay their taxes on time and increase the amount they have for personal expenses from $38,830 to $39,260.

Best of all, they could do it all with no psychological stress, since their tracking system is in place and operational. They know exactly how they are progressing month by month and what adjustments, if any, need to be made. In short, they have a very specific plan, and they are in control. It's a very empowering approach that tends to build both self-esteem and self-confidence.

PREPARING YOUR IDEAL SCENE
FOR CASH FLOW

Before you begin completing Your Ideal Scene for Cash Flow for the coming year, we suggest that you carefully review your Current Cash Flow form. Is your annual net at least 10 percent of your total income? If it is, then you're well on your way to establishing Financial Freedom. You're generating assets that we hope you are investing wisely and that will be available to you when you want or need them. For you, a Financial Freedom program can result in an *even greater* surplus of money, which you will be free to use as you like.

If, on the other hand, you're not adding to your Wealth-Building Account by at least 10 percent of your total income, it's important to consider changing your financial habits in accordance with one of the following strategies, which were first mentioned in chapter 6, "A Quest for Balance." For you, a Financial Freedom program is essential for launching you on the road to wealth. Remember, one of the primary goals of your Financial Freedom program is for you to learn to manage your money so that you have at least 10 percent more cash coming in every month than is going out!

How?

Approach #1. Increase your income.

Approach #2. Decrease your expenses.

Approach #3. Increase your income *and* decrease your expenses.

Discovering which approach will work best for you can be a wonderful opportunity for challenging your creativity. As you implement your chosen strategy, you'll have the satisfaction of knowing you are increasing your wealth and Financial Freedom. You'll be running your financial kingdom rather than being run by it!

GET ON THE PATH TO WEALTH

This process has amazing snowball effects. By instituting the Financial Freedom program, you're literally retraining your Private

Access Learning System (PALS) to always be increasing your wealth. You're laying down the track that will carry you along the path to wealth. And the more you do it, the more of a habit it becomes. With the Banks family's examples, there was nothing outrageous and certainly nothing that wasn't at least 50 percent believable.

Can it possibly be that something in your consciousness really knows which stocks are going up and will choose those once you've trained it to advise you? Sometimes it sure seems that way! If an Olympic skier trains his PALS to assist him in becoming a world champion athlete, you can train your PALS to assist you to be a *financial* champion! We're doing it, we've seen others do it, and you can do it, too. The process will actually energize you. So have fun while you train your PALS for success!

ACTION STEPS ～～～～～～～～～～～～～～～～～

1. Refer to your Current Assets form.

2. Taking your time, complete your form for Your Ideal Scene for Assets (page 234) for the beginning of the next year or, if it's currently late in the year, for the beginning of the year after.

3. Place a copy of the completed form in the folder you've created called "Ideal Scenes and Already There Reports."

4. Next complete your form for Your Ideal Scene for Cash Flow (page 235); place the completed form in the "Ideal Scenes and Already There Reports" folder.

5. Make an appointment with yourself to read chapter 20, "Want Financial Success? You're Already There!" Keep the appointment.

6. Go to a mirror right now and appreciate yourself for taking a significant step in consciously engaging and directing the creative part of yourself.

WANT FINANCIAL
SUCCESS? YOU'RE
ALREADY THERE!

Now it's time to anchor your Ideal Scenes even more firmly in reality with a powerful method we call Already There Reports.

Learning this method allows you to maximize the time and energy that you put into the creative part of your program for getting rich.

All you need to do to create an Already There Report is take an Ideal Scene and write about it as if you were *already there*—with it occurring *right now!* Taking one of your Ideal Scenes and describing it as if it were financial reality is a very powerful way to further clarify, energize and anchor your Ideal Scene. If an Ideal Scene is a snapshot of what we envision our financial life to be, an Already There Report is a movie enlivened with the energy that comes with enthusiastic animation.

We've developed two samples: one based on the **186** Banks Family's Ideal Scene for Assets, and the other based on the Banks Family's Ideal Scene for Cash Flow. But before we share them with you, here are four helpful guidelines for creating your own Already There Reports.

1. Be immediate. Write in the first person, present tense. The only time we really live is *now*. It's never a week from now or a week ago, it's always *now*. Reality is now, in *this* moment. So to make your Already There Reports *real*, you must write them as if they were happening right now. If you talk about them as future happenings, the creative part of you relegates them to the future, which makes them less immediate or urgent. But if you talk about them as if they were happening *now*, your creative mind experiences them as if they were really happening now. Your mind then goes about turning them into reality—*now*. The more you act like something is real, the sooner it becomes reality.

2. Energize yourself. You can add energy to your reports with vivid, descriptive language and enthusiasm. Have you ever noticed that the more you really get into something, the better your results tend to be? Ideal Scenes and Already There Reports are tools we use to make a commitment to future wealth—but we need energy to create the reality. The richer your imagery and the more enthusiasm you put into it, the more energy you have available for creating.

3. Put yourself in the picture. We recently went on a wonderful trip to the Canadian Rockies and spent a good deal of time hiking in the mountains. Some of our favorite hikes were to fantastically beautiful alpine meadows, where, being good tourists, we shot many rolls of film. Some were of scenery only, but more had scenery plus one or both of us. When we returned home, developed our pictures and showed them to friends, we realized we could talk with much more animation about the pictures that had *us* in them.

It's one thing to say "Here's a picture of Angel Glacier from Cavell Meadows." It's another altogether to be able to say "Here we are in Cavell Meadows, and you can see Angel Glacier behind us. You wouldn't believe what it was like to hike up there in the rain." Putting yourself in the picture is another way of enlivening your Already There Reports with creative energy and helping them become more believable to you.

4. Express your gratitude. Keeping things in perspective is psychologically healthy. If you're going to put energy into increasing your wealth, you also want to remember to express gratitude for what you already have as well as for what you are currently receiving. This is one of the primary ways of staying at peace with your finances.

For many people, writing Already There Reports on their Ideal Scenes is a way of more fully bringing their vision alive. It becomes a story, not just a collection of numbers.

You can use these Already There Reports from the Banks family as models for creating your own.

ALREADY THERE REPORT FOR ASSETS: THE RICH AND GOLDIE BANKS COMPANY

"It's January 1, 1994, and we're happily reviewing our family's financial assets. We're celebrating the success of our efforts in easily and naturally implementing our Financial Freedom program, and we're very grateful for all we've received.

"Our certificate of deposit has grown more than $1,200 and is now worth more than $28,300! We're taking this money and investing it in the Abundance Growth Fund (or another highly profitable investment), which currently pays at least a 7 percent dividend and has the potential of increasing in stock shares per year by more than 5 percent! We're easily and naturally increasing our wealth, living our dreams and wisely using our assets to uplift ourselves and other people!

"Our home not only provides a wonderful space for us to live and raise our children, our home equity has increased in value from $23,000 to more than $28,000! We're glad we purchased this home, making this investment in ourselves and our family. We take care of our home and property and enjoy maintaining and improving the house and yard. We know this is an appreciating asset that's an important part of our wealth-building program.

"Our mail-order business is mushrooming! Satisfied customers are telling others about our products, and sales are increasing! Our products are high quality and are in demand! The business is steady, and a positive growth trend has been established. The value of the business has increased from $36,000 six months ago to more than $40,000 now! This business is becoming so profitable that we anticipate it easily and generously funding our children's education and our retirement!

"We like having cash on hand! It reinforces our experience of abundance and wealth! We just counted our current cash on hand and are delighted to find that we now have over $600!

"Our automobiles provide us with safe, reliable transportation. We own one free and clear, and the other is almost paid off! Our cars are in excellent condition, and we practice preventive maintenance, which is paying dividends. Our cars have retained their value. In checking prices for comparable used cars, the value of our cars is still about $11,700!

"One of the benefits our business provides for us is our life insurance policy! It feels good to provide for and protect our children in the event of something unexpected. And in checking the current cash surrender value of the policy, we're happy to see that it has increased to well over $3,000! We're investigating term insurance and researching the advantages and disadvantages of both types of coverage for our family. We enjoy using our financial resources wisely, providing abundantly for our needs now and in the future!

"This Financial Freedom program is really working! Our marketable securities have increased by over 25 percent! When we checked with our broker, he said, 'You guys really picked a couple of winners when you invested in these!' We've done our homework and regularly tracked the buy-and-sell prices of these investments. They just keep on gaining in value. Way to go!

"We're continually evaluating the current information on these investments to determine whether it is best to continue to hold these stocks because they still have significant growth potential or whether it's best to sell them, successfully reinvesting our profits in another low-risk security with greater potential.

"Our personal property is easily increasing in value! We love the lithographs we own, and in addition, our favorite artist is becoming more well known and has had several shows in national galleries! Our art collection is appreciating in value. We're happy we now have extra money to buy another small litho at a fabulous price! Our personal property has increased in value to more than $7,550!

"We love planning for the future! We're committed to putting money in our individual retirement account (IRA) each year. In fact, both of us have an IRA, and we easily fund them annually!

"We're always open to receiving happy financial surprises! When we look at the 'Windfall' line in our Ideal Scene, we smile, knowing that both our hearts and our minds are open to receiving magic. We know that happy financial surprises can come at any time. We're always open to receiving even greater financial prosperity!

"In reviewing our assets and totaling the increase, we joyfully acknowledge that our assets have easily increased more than $20,000 in the past six months! This is an increase of over 15 percent! We've been empowered by taking charge of our financial kingdom! Getting actively involved in our Financial Freedom program on a regular basis has really helped us increase our wealth.

"We're now creating our Ideal Scene for Assets for 1995. It is fun and easy! We work well together! We're enjoying the process of using the Financial Freedom program to support us in getting rich! Our assets continue to grow, and we are grateful.

"This or something better for the highest good of all concerned."

ALREADY THERE REPORT FOR CASH FLOW: THE RICH AND GOLDIE BANKS COMPANY

"We are super-excited to be able to say 'Yes, Rich and Goldie Banks are *really* doing it! We *are* indeed living in positive cash flow!'

"Our income and our expenses are in balance, and we easily continue going ahead, increasing our wealth by 10 percent or more of our total income each year.

"We enjoy paying ourselves *first* each month and find that we can easily pay ourselves 10 percent or more of our gross income and still have more than enough to provide for ourselves and our children while paying our bills on time. We're so glad we learned about paying ourselves first! We are experiencing firsthand the power of paying ourselves first while practicing the skills of money management and building wealth!

"It's January 1, 1994, and we're reviewing our income and expense records. Because we've been keeping our records current every month, we already know the good news! We are happy campers and are having a special celebration today to acknowledge our success and express our gratitude for the work we're doing to establish and maintain a healthy cash flow!

"On the income side, I—Rich—received the raise I was anticipating. In fact, my supervisors have been so pleased with my work that I'm told that I am being considered for a promotion that means an additional substantial salary increase. And, surprise, surprise, the company is doing so well, I received an unexpected bonus—the gift of a block of stock certificates during the holidays! The company management recognizes the value of all employees 'owning' a share in the business. Our family's income has increased by over 10 percent, and my gross annual salary is now at $40,000 or more!

"Our mail-order business is taking off! By simply establishing and holding our intention to increase earnings, we reached nearly $20,000 this past year! Our customers love our products, and 80 percent of our current customers reorder! We're building a loyal and satisfied customer base and a profitable business that will easily fund our retirement and our children's education!

"All the interest and dividends we received during this past year have remained in our Wealth-Building Account. No interest or dividends have been used to pay expenses. Instead, we've added them completely to our assets.

"We're grateful for our commitment to our Financial Freedom program and our goal of continuously increasing our wealth! Our focus is paying handsome rewards!

"We love looking at the 'Gifts' and 'Windfall' lines on our Ideal Scene because they remind us that unexpected happy financial surprises can come at any time. While we're not attached to any particular outcome, we *are* open to receiving even greater financial prosperity.

"On the expense side, we've faithfully paid ourselves 10 percent or more of our gross income! And we've done this with grace and ease! A piece of cake!

"We love paying ourselves first. It's such a demonstration of our caring for ourselves and our financial future! We're enjoying the process of increasing our wealth. We've become wise stewards of all our resources, including our financial riches. Also, we know we're teaching our children by example about living in positive cash flow and creating wealth.

"We're so delighted that we've successfully expanded sales in our business with only a moderate increase in expenses. We've both been willing to work more hours in the business during evenings and weekends as part of our commitment to living in positive cash flow! That way, we don't have the added expense of hiring other employees. Our willingness to go for it has produced the results we want, and our annual business expenses are less than $4,000.

"Every month we've been placing money in our tax accrual savings account. When we knew our income would be increasing, we contacted our accountant, who advised us how much we'd need to set aside for federal and state income tax as well as for state disability insurance. This has really helped us plan ahead. We know we've set aside enough in our tax savings account to easily pay our taxes when they're due in April! And in the meantime, we're earning interest on the money! We sleep well at night, knowing that our tax obligations are handled.

"Since living in positive cash flow is important to us, we carefully monitor our level of indebtedness each month. Our monthly projections call for debt reduction of a minimum of $150 per month. We're easily paying down our debt at this rate or faster. By reducing debt and paying our bills on time, we're increasing our own wealth rather than helping build the wealth of credit card companies. We can see the day when we'll be debt-free, and we give thanks for our willingness to eliminate debt and develop the financial habits that support us in living in positive cash flow!

"We've completed our 1993 Annual Expense Summary Spreadsheet, and we're delighted to see that our spending is in line with our projections. We're grateful that we have a comfortable home, plenty to eat, nice clothing, safe, reliable transportation and more than enough money to cover our current desires and aspirations.

"Tracking our income and expenses every month has helped us monitor our spending and make appropriate 'course corrections' as needed in a relaxed yet conscious way!

"We've maintained a satisfactory standard of living, and perhaps even more important, the quality of our life has improved as we've worked together, implementing our Financial Freedom program and increasing our wealth.

"We have goals and aspirations! We're dreaming bigger dreams than we did before! And we're putting foundations under those dreams now. Our working together in this way has deepened our relationship, and we're closer now.

"Right now, we're making our Ideal Scene for Cash Flow for next year. We're using last year's figures to assist us in establishing workable projections for the coming year. And we're enjoying ourselves immensely!

"This or something better for the highest good of all concerned."

ACTION STEPS

1. Refer to your Ideal Scenes for Assets.

2. Bring forward your enthusiasm, and write an energizing and uplifting Already There Report for your assets.

3. Once you've got the hang of it, write another Already There Report for your cash flow.

4. File your reports in your folder labeled "Ideal Scenes and Already There Reports."

5. Consider making an audiocassette recording of yourself enthusiastically reading your Already There Reports. Then you can play them in the car each day or when you're working around the house. It's a great way to inwardly anchor what you intend to create in your financial kingdom.

6. Make an appointment with yourself to read chapter 21, "The Power Tools for Building Wealth," and keep it.

THE POWER TOOLS
FOR BUILDING
WEALTH

If you've ever built anything, you know the importance of choosing the right tools. You wouldn't try to use a screwdriver to cut wood any more than you'd attempt to use a saw to hammer in a nail.

In the same way, you need the right tools for working effectively in your *mind*, where all creative ideas are first evaluated by your Private Access Learning System (PALS).

You've already developed two powerful tools for working with your PALS—Ideal Scenes and Already There Reports. What you need next are super-duper tools that uproot the old habits of limited thinking that can sabotage your new efforts. Not only that, these power tools then replace the old stuff with new beliefs and perceptions that support you in becoming wealthy.

The psychological term for these tools is *anchoring*.

"Anchoring" means grounding, securing or stabi-

194 lizing your new mental beliefs, which support wealth-building behavior. When new attitudes and actions are accepted by your PALS and become anchored in your consciousness, you've created brand-new habits.

Anchoring is mental exercise. As with anchoring's physical counterpart—pumping iron—repetition is very important. Just as you systematically exercise physical muscles (doing reps), you must learn to systematically exercise your mental muscles—your beliefs and thoughts. This strengthens and supports beneficial new behavior designed to increase your wealth.

What's the "iron" you'll pump in your mind? Your Ideal Scenes and Already There Reports. In this chapter, we'll show you how to use those weights—with proper anchoring—to maximum benefit.

Think of this as "pumping gold"—your personalized training program for becoming wealthy.

To start, we'll tell you about the anchoring techniques that can positively affect your finances in the shortest possible time.

ANCHORING BY REVIEW

This technique is the easiest to do and works best with your Ideal Scenes. All it involves is enthusiastically reviewing your Ideal Scenes regularly. Each time you go over them, you're powerfully anchoring your intention to create wealth by instructing your PALS: "This is my new financial reality." Through this process, you are literally changing your beliefs about what is true for you.

Remember what we said earlier: *Energy follows thought.* What you tell yourself tends to become your reality. By looking over your Ideal Scenes with enthusiasm, you're instructing your PALS to manifest these *mental* pictures in the *physical* world. You're clearly telling your PALS exactly where you want to be financially in one year.

Sound too simple? Don't take our word for it. Dare to experiment by doing what we're suggesting and find out for yourself!

Sound too far out, kind of like UFOs and the Loch Ness monster? This information might be totally new to you, so we want to emphasize that we're teaching a very practical, down-to-earth approach to money. Its power comes from a sound psychological principle: The clearer you are in your mind about what you want, the more likely you are to create it.

To demonstrate this principle, here are two scenarios. You decide which one is more likely to motivate you in the direction of financial well-being.

In the first, you *sense* that you really should spend less on clothes and eating out because you'd like to have a nice vacation and a money surplus at the end of the year.

In the second, you *know* that to accomplish your financial goals for the year, you must trim $250 from your "clothes" and "eating out" categories while increasing your "vacation" category by $100 a month. That will give you a net increase in savings of $150 a month or $1,800 a year.

In the first instance, all you have is a vague sense of where you want to be. You can't effectively plan your vacation, since you don't know whether you'll be able to afford it. And if you don't even know if you're spending too much for a shirt or blouse, you *certainly won't know* if you're living in positive cash flow, breaking even or going into debt.

In the second scenario, you know exactly what your options are as well as the consequences. You can see it clearly and experience it in your mind's eye. You know how much you can spend on clothes and eating out. You also know exactly how much you'll have for your vacation. This adds a psychological bonus: You have more fun—instead of stress—planning your trip, since you know it's in total harmony with your financial goals. Best of all, you know you're increasing your wealth by $1,800 a year.

Which approach do you think will better motivate you to achieve your goals?

No spaceships, no Nessie, no unsolved mysteries.

(*Note:* In the next chapter, we'll tell you how to implement your own personal Financial Freedom program—including information on where to keep your Ideal Scenes and Already There Reports and how often and how long to review them.)

ANCHORING BY MENTAL REHEARSAL

Mental rehearsal, also known as visualization, is an even more powerful technique for you to use to anchor your dreams in reality. As we've said, recent research indicates that the human biocomputer doesn't seem to differentiate all that well between a physical event and the clear imagining of that event.

Said another way, your PALS tend to treat imagined events in much the same way as actual events. When you mentally rehearse the way you want something to be, your PALS begin to go about creating that event in the physical world. Every time you visualize your Ideal Scenes or Already There Reports, you're redefining reality to your PALS. Sooner or later, your new definition *becomes* reality.

This is not a theory. We've seen it work thousands of times.

When asked during an interview how it was that his shots were so accurate, a famous world-class golfer told how he'd step up to the tee and, before swinging his club, he'd visualize a perfect swing and see the ball sailing down the fairway—a perfect shot.

This practice of mental rehearsal is used by almost all professional and Olympic athletes of every nation. It's entering the business and medical communities as well. Corporate boards of directors and chief executive officers report meetings where, eyes closed, they visualize their sales increasing, their factories running smoothly or their union relations improving. Patients overcoming health conditions are taught stress reduction by imagining themselves strolling through a peaceful forest.

Anchoring by mental rehearsal is a tailor-made technique for use with your Already There Reports. Again, the key to success is to use the technique regularly and enthusiastically (think "reps"). The more creative energy you can bring to the visualization, the more effective you'll be at manifesting it. Actually see yourself in the scenario as if it were happening right now. What will you be saying? How will you be feeling? You can imagine yourself writing a significant check, paying off a loan, successfully settling a long-standing debt or placing the key in the front door of your brand-new home, turning it and hearing that beautiful click as the door opens.

Often people find it helpful to close their eyes when they visualize so that they can better concentrate. If you're not used to doing this, you might be very pleasantly surprised at how much fun it can be. It's like the commercial: "Try it. You'll like it!" Experiment and find out what works best for you. And remember: There's no wrong way to do it, unless, of course, you simply choose not to do it at all.

ANCHORING BY AFFIRMATION

A third technique for anchoring is through the use of affirmations—sentences you tell yourself that positively reinforce the outcome you're seeking to achieve. Affirmations are actually powerful statements of clear intention. While reviewing your Ideal Scene for Cash Flow, for example, you might be saying inwardly "I am easily and naturally increasing my cash flow by $200 or more each month." Say the affirmation several times daily with enthusiasm, and use several different affirmations. Develop some for each category in your Ideal Scene for Assets and your Ideal Scene for Cash Flow. You might want to have some general affirmations as well, along the lines of "I am abundantly wealthy."

Affirmations are another way of letting your PALS know what you want to achieve. While anchoring by review and by mental rehearsal are visually oriented, anchoring by affirmations provides direct instructions. Remember, in your universe, your word is law! We've found that affirmations work best when they're done with a recognition that you're working to create greater abundance on several levels. You aren't simply raising your standard of living. You're enhancing the quality of life for yourself and your family. For this reason, we often add "This or something better for the highest good of all concerned" at the end of our affirmations.

Some affirmations for increasing your wealth that we've found to be very inspirational are:

"Abundance is my natural state of being."

"I am earning a great income doing what satisfies me."

"I am open and receptive to new avenues of income."

"Every dollar I spend returns to me multiplied."

"I am a successful manager of money, and my efforts are paying off handsomely."

"Every day I am growing more financially prosperous."

"I am healthy, wealthy and wise."

"Financial success is coming to me easily and naturally."

"I am a prospering person, wisely using my abundant assets to uplift myself and others."

"I am giving to others from my abundance; it pays to be generous."

"I am a wonderful and successful person, living in positive cash flow."

"I am wisely investing money in those areas that produce large and timely financial returns."

"I am joyfully sharing and gratefully receiving the abundant riches of the universe."

"I am rejoicing in others' successes, knowing that there is plenty for all."

"I am freely giving and receiving."

"I am successfully practicing Financial Freedom; positive cash flow and increasing assets are my reward."

One very effective way we've found to work with affirmations is to make what is known as an endless loop cassette tape. You can buy these tapes at most places that sell telephone answering machines. Get the three-minute variety. You can record your affirmations along with any instrumental music you feel will help motivate you. And they'll keep playing over and over until you stop the tape.

When recording your tape, say the affirmation twice. Then when you play it, you'll hear the affirmation once and then say it aloud with enthusiasm the second time. Listening to and saying your affirmations really works great on those long drives between work and home. You can play the tape over and over for as long as you wish. The more you play it, the more you are directly instructing your PALS about how you'd like your financial reality to be.

ANCHORING BY HEURISTICS

Our favorite anchoring technique involves a process with a long history. Heuristics are objects or images that constantly remind you of what's important. For instance, Catholics pray a rosary, and Jews wear yarmulkes on their heads. In both cases, the essential purpose of these heuristics is to remind the people of the presence of God.

Heuristic comes from an ancient Greek word meaning "to discover" or "to point out." We use it psychologically to mean "to remind" or "to bring into awareness."

We have a variety of playful heuristics that remind us of our financial goals and aspirations. One of our favorites is a small glass globe similar to the kind you probably had as a kid—it snowed inside when you turned it upside down. Well, the one we have has a label with my (Ron's) name placed at the bottom front, and in the middle sits a very prosperous-looking gentleman with his arms reaching upward. When you invert it, instead of white snow, an abundance of greenbacks pours down on the man—a great reminder of our financial goals and aspirations.

Another one of our favorites is a one-ounce Canadian maple leaf gold coin. We just love the feel of it. Some coin collectors have told us that every time we rub it, we're actually rubbing away some of the gold. But to us, the coin is like Aladdin's magic lamp. When we rub it, we can almost see the genie of wealth blessing us.

Some other heuristics we use include pads that are printed as thousand-dollar bills on one side and a model of a Rolls Royce automobile with a picture of the two of us in the front seat. *Anything* that brings wealth to your awareness will work as a heuristic to anchor your intention for greater prosperity in your mind—from luxurious clothing to a beautiful work of art.

At times, we've developed heuristics for specific financial goals. When we wanted to go to Hawaii and vacation at a particular resort, we got a copy of a gorgeous ad for the hotel, including a photo of its beautiful oval swimming pool with an orchid inlaid in tile on the bottom. We cut out pictures of our faces and put them on the heads of the couple appearing in the ad. Then we hung the ad on our refrigerator door, where we'd see it several times a day—always anchoring our intention and programming us to make this vacation a reality.

Guess where we vacationed the next summer?

That's right. We enjoyed a spectacular Hawaiian holiday, including a delightful stay at that beautiful, luxurious resort and several great swims in the orchid pool.

Many of our clients and seminar participants have used these techniques as well. One that's been quite successful involves taking a picture of yourself, for example, in front of your dream home as a way of anchoring your intention to purchase such a home for yourself and your family. Once again, this simple step is a very powerful way of supporting yourself in achieving your goals.

DREAMS REALLY DO COME TRUE

Here's a story from Mary.

Ever since I was a little girl, I dreamed of going to Europe. My most special fantasy was to go to Switzerland and see the Matterhorn. As I grew older, I made several friends whose families came from Scandinavia. They'd always tell me how beautiful the Scandinavian countries are. So my European fantasy began to include Scandinavia as well as Switzerland.

I carried this dream into my adult years.

In the early years of our marriage, Ron and I decided to make my dream come true. We planned our ideal trip to Scandinavia with a side trip to Switzerland. We created an Ideal Scene and Already There Report. We began our mental rehearsals. Of course, we started saying appropriate affirmations.

As it got closer to the summer during which we were "supposed" to go, we realized that we didn't really have the time and that the cost was more than our financial program could adequately handle.

And so we let go of the idea.

Except for me.

I just quietly kept up my mental rehearsals, simply substituting "next summer" for "this summer." I stayed with my internal program for creating my European dream trip.

One summer day, we arrived at our office to find a letter from Norway. A fellow educator—someone we didn't know—had heard about our work and wanted to know if, by any chance, we had any interest in coming to Norway "next summer" to conduct two seminars on counseling skills for a group of Norwegian counselors, educators and consultants.

Of course, he said, they'd pay our fee, plus all our traveling expenses.

Yikes! My dream was appearing right before my eyes!

The next summer, we indeed had a wonderful time in Norway, touring some of the most beautiful countryside in the world.

And of course, we flew from Norway to Switzerland to make my childhood dream of seeing the Matterhorn come true!

Oh yes, as a result of the money we earned conducting the seminars, our entire first-class, three-week European fantasy trip cost us nothing. The expense matched the income—and we didn't have to adjust any categories in our Financial Freedom program to accommodate the trip.

You can see why we call these "power tools." They really work, and they can work *fast*.

Now it's time to begin developing yours.

ACTION STEPS 〰〰〰〰〰〰〰〰〰〰〰〰〰

1. Begin developing a set of financial affirmations and actually write them down. You may want to incorporate some of the ones we've suggested in this chapter. Another excellent source is the true/false test you completed on page 50. Take any question that you answered "true" and change that question into a positive statement. Then make that statement into an affirmation.

For example, let's go back to our true/false test. If you checked statement 19 as at least partially true, you believe that to make a lot of money, you have to be dishonest and do illegal things. Changing that to a positive statement might go something like this: "It's certainly possible to make lots of money honestly and legally." The affirmation is: "I am making huge sums of money ethically, legally, honestly and with integrity."

2. Identify and collect some fun heuristics to have around you when you're in your "financial headquarters." In fact, some heuristics, like a gold coin or a hundred-dollar bill, you can carry with you throughout the day.

3. You're doing great. Only two chapters to go, so make an appointment with yourself to read chapter 22, "Eight Minutes a Day That Will Change Your Life." Keep that appointment.

CHAPTER *22*

EIGHT MINUTES A DAY THAT WILL CHANGE YOUR LIFE

Eight minutes doesn't sound like a lot of time to get a job done. What can you really do in eight minutes? Boil an egg? Maybe. Jog a mile? On a *good* day, pal. Convince your two-year-old to let you put on his *other* shoe? Forget it.

But we've got some really good news about what you positively *can* get done in eight minutes.

And it's something so powerful, it can be life altering.

Our research shows that if you spend as little as eight minutes a day in creative anchoring activity, you can keep your powerful Private Access Learning System (PALS) on target to create wealth.

Imagine, only eight minutes! Just 480 little seconds!

Of course, that eight minutes is a minimum—feel free to do more.

What's really critical is that you do your anchoring systematically and consistently. In other words, at least eight minutes *every day* for maximum effect.

Your *attitude* while doing your eight minutes a day is extremely important. The more you can relax while keeping an enthusiastic and positive mental focus, the more you'll create an internal environment for wealth to flourish.

Here's our suggestion for beginning your daily eight-minute mental program for financial success. After you've worked with it for a while, you may want to vary the amount of time you spend on each activity.

REVIEW YOUR IDEAL SCENES (TWO MINUTES A DAY)

Let's start with your Ideal Scenes for Assets and Cash Flow that you've created for one year from now.

We suggest that you simply review your Ideal Scenes a minimum of *once a day for one minute each.* Please *do not* try to study or memorize them. Instead, have *fun* just looking them over. Enjoy yourself! This enthusiastic energy helps anchor your intention to live in positive cash flow and to increase your wealth.

It's very important to review your Ideal Scenes one at a time as if they were your current financial reality—that's right, as if today is really one year from now and you are, indeed, as wealthy as your Ideal Scenes say you are.

Focus on your new wealth while relaxing and enjoying the process, knowing that every time you look over your Ideal Scenes, you're actually helping to make them real. Each minute you spend in enthusiastic review helps direct your PALS to reprogram your mental "wealth tape" so that abundance is yours.

If you start feeling excited or happy during your review, that's wonderful. Remember, enthusiasm and joy supply energy boosts to help your money dreams come true.

Our research shows that the key to success by anchoring is *consistency.* It's far more powerful to invest 1 minute per day *every day* than to let a month slip by and then do 30 minutes all at once. Some of our clients have been very creative in making sure they review their Ideal Scenes daily. In fact, one woman laminated her Ideal Scenes and hung them in her shower! Every day, she'd spend her shower time enjoying her Ideal Scenes.

Other people make reduced photocopies of their Ideal Scenes

so that they can keep them in their daily appointment books. This can be an excellent way to fill up a few minutes while you're waiting for an appointment—and it's great way to be productive while you're on hold on the phone. The more you look over your Ideal Scenes, the more you're reeducating your PALS.

But remember, even if you glance at them several times during the day, you still want to have a minimum of one full minute of *uninterrupted, relaxed and concentrated reviewing* for each Ideal Scene every day.

VISUALIZE YOUR ALREADY THERE REPORTS (THREE MINUTES A DAY)

The most important point to remember about visualization is that it's *not* the same as daydreaming. There's nothing random and unfocused about these mental rehearsals. Instead, you're consciously directing your PALS to let you "see" the financial goals you've stated in your Already There Reports. Remaining relaxed yet focused will help a lot.

Be sure to see yourself clearly in the mental rehearsal. For example, imagine yourself walking to the bank to deposit that check for $1,000. What are you wearing? What street are you on? Is the sun shining? Is there a cool breeze? Noisy traffic? Chirping birds?

Remember: A mental rehearsal is *not* static—it's not a picture frozen in time, like a photograph. Instead, you should feel like you're watching a live-action *movie*—one in which you're the writer, director, producer and *star!*

We suggest that you allocate a minimum of *three minutes every day* for this part of your program. Like your Ideal Scenes, the more often you visualize your success, the more you're reprogramming your mind to support you in increasing your wealth.

ENERGIZE YOUR AFFIRMATIONS (THREE MINUTES A DAY)

Two great benefits of affirmations are their flexibility and ease of use. You can say them out loud or silently to yourself. You can say them while driving to and from your work. And as we've said, you can make a cassette tape of yourself saying them, with beautiful music in the background, and listen to them as you drive, exercise or even fall asleep.

We've made several different kinds of affirmation tapes. One of our favorites has very upbeat music, with us loudly and enthusiastically affirming in the background. And you can make separate tapes for your Ideal Scene for Assets, your Ideal Scene for Cash Flow, your Already There Reports and your affirmations. It's extremely empowering!

Every time you say your affirmations, you're instructing your PALS in a reeducation process that brings each affirmation closer to physical reality.

Remember: The more enthusiasm and joy you put into your affirmations, the better this process works.

Once again, we suggest that you do your affirmations a minimum of *three minutes every day.* And that's three minutes all at one time so that the energy of your enthusiasm can build while you're saying them. You can enrich the experience of saying your affirmations by playing with your heuristics at the same time. Have fun playing with your wealth symbols. Rub a gold coin, hold hundred-dollar bills and smile, browse through a brochure for your dream vacation. And remember, keep focused on your enthusiasm and joy.

DAILY STRATEGIES FOR CREATING WEALTH: THE RICH AND GOLDIE BANKS COMPANY

You have many options to choose from in creating your eight-minute-a-day program (or should we say *re*program). On page 236, you'll find a new worksheet designed to help you succeed. We call it: Daily Strategies for Creating Wealth.

As an example of how to use this handy tool every day, let's check in with our pals Rich and Goldie Banks. You'll find their Daily Strategies sheet on page 208. As you can see, the anchoring activities are listed in two categories: "One-Minute-a-Day Choices" and "Three-Minute-a-Day Choices."

How does this work?

Much like the oft-repeated line about ordering from a Chinese restaurant menu: "Take one from column A and two from column B." Only in this case, *each day* Rich and Goldie choose at least two anchoring activities from the "One-Minute-a-Day Choices" column and at least two from the "Three-Minute-a-Day Choices" column. That satisfies their minimum daily requirement to maintain their powerful mental reprogramming to developing wealth.

To keep track of their anchoring, Rich and Goldie check off their activity of choice every day in the boxes provided.

On page 236, you'll find a blank worksheet. This is *your* Daily Strategies for Creating Wealth form. Fill in the activities—both one- and three-minute choices—that you want to participate in. Then mix and match your choices daily to meet your eight-minute minimum.

In doing these strategies for reprogramming your PALS, you are *consciously* taking control of your own financial destiny. Give yourself a great big pat on the back. Most people spend their entire lives *unconscious* about their money. That's why 93 percent of them end up totally unprepared for retirement—dependent on the government, charity and family.

You do *not* have to be one of them. Instead, you can become completely responsible for creating a life of abundance, prosperity and riches.

Enthusiastically investing at least eight minutes a day in your future is one key to your success.

We think you're worth it. Don't you?

THE BANKS FAMILY'S DAILY STRATEGIES FOR CREATING WEALTH

ONE-MINUTE-A-DAY CHOICES	M	T	W	Th	F	Sa	Su
1. Review your reasons for wanting to be wealthy.							
2. Review your Ideal Scene for Assets. Have fun seeing your assets growing!							
3. Review your Ideal Scene for Cash Flow. Visualize yourself easily and naturally living in positive cash flow!							
4. Acknowledge and appreciate yourself and your willingness to be wealthy.							
5. Visualize yourself living debt-free! See yourself easily and naturally bringing forward the resources to pay all debts!							
6. Give thanks for the abundance already present in your life.							
7. Enjoy playing with your heuristic!							
THREE-MINUTE-A-DAY CHOICES							
1. Visualize yourself as wealthy as you want to be.							
2. Enthusiastically say your affirmations in the shower, in the car when you're driving, when you're waiting for an appointment, etc.							
3. Review your Already There Reports, seeing yourself living your dream!							
4. Express appreciations to yourself and those around you who are cooperating with you in successfully implementing your Financial Freedom program!							
5. Look in the mirror and share loving, nurturing, positive self-talk with yourself about you and your finances.							
6. Engage in compassionate self-forgiveness for any judgments you've placed against yourself having to do with money and finances.							

CHAPTER
23

BEGIN IT NOW!

In our work with people over the years, we've witnessed something almost miraculous happen to some ordinary, everyday folks. This extraordinary phenomenon is usually familiar only to champion athletes and other people who function at high levels of achievement. But the good news is that it's also available to *you*.

What is it?

We call it magic.

But it's a very specific kind of magic. It happens only when you dare to begin taking positive action about something you want—like increased wealth.

Seemingly out of nowhere, wonderful things begin to happen to you.

What we're talking about is best summed up in the following quote from William Hutchison Murray, a Scottish mountaineer who wrote about his challenging Himalayan adventures.

> *Until one is committed, there is hesitancy, the chance to draw back, always ineffectiveness.*
> *Concerning all acts of initiative (and creation), there is one elementary truth, the ignorance of*

*which kills countless ideas and splendid plans: that the mo-
ment one definitely commits oneself, then Providence moves,
too.*

*All sorts of things occur to help one that would never other-
wise have occurred. A whole stream of events issues from the
decision, raising in one's favor all manner of unforeseen inci-
dents and meetings and material assistance, which no man
could have dreamt would have come his way.*

THE POWER OF POSITIVE HABITS

One of the things we do almost every day is walk. But we don't
just stroll leisurely on the beach. We practice fitness walking,
which involves walking fast enough to elevate our heart rates to a
certain level and then walking at that rate for at least 20 minutes.

However, there's something special about walking that goes far
beyond the physical benefits. Walking makes us feel good about
ourselves. When we set a goal—like regularly going for a brisk
walk—and we actually do it, we're filled with a feeling of success
and accomplishment.

The bottom-line benefit of a brisk walk?

Not only a healthy elevation of our heart rates but *a sensa-
tional elevation of our self-esteem!* With this kind of reinforcement, we find that walking one day leads to walking the next day,
and the next . . . and the next. And that's what it takes for us to establish a positive habit.

In exactly the same way, if you save $200 one month, that can
lead to $200 the next month, and the next. Before too long, you'll
establish a positive habit for yourself: accumulating money!

Our essential message is this: Earning more than you spend is
a positive habit that conditions your mind to support you in continuing to amass wealth. The psychological result of building up
wealth is a feeling of accomplishment, mastery and success. The
financial result is prosperity, abundance and riches.

KEEPING TRACK OF YOUR MILLION-DOLLAR COMPANY

Here's a fact of the business world that you might not know:
All well-managed companies prepare a monthly statement as a
way of monitoring revenues, expenses and cash flow.

What does this have to do with your personal finances? Well, as President of your own million-dollar company, you're responsible for preparing your *own* personal monthly statement. Why? Because having accurate facts and figures about your money empowers and assists you in staying on track with your mission: paying yourself first and always increasing your wealth by at least 10 percent of your income each month.

We suggest that you start by setting aside *a couple of hours every other week* for your tracking activities. We've found that it's far better to set aside a specific time on a regular basis than to do it "when I have a few minutes."

What will you do during this special time?

This time is devoted to tracking your finances through Your Personal Money Management System. You'll be involved in activities such as: entering your income on your Annual Income Summary Spreadsheet, paying yourself first, paying your bills, completing your Monthly Expense Spreadsheet, recording your Monthly Expense Spreadsheet totals on your Annual Expense Summary Spreadsheet, keeping your checkbook up-to-date, reconciling your bank statement, evaluating whether your expenditures are above or below your monthly projections, tracking debt reduction, tracking the progress of your investments and getting your records together for income tax preparation.

We know that right now some of you are thinking "Where am I going to get an extra couple of hours?"

In our work with financial clients, we've found that most people are already spending *considerably more time* than what we're suggesting just trying to keep up with, keep track of or even make sense of their money situation. These are all things you're already spending time doing—you're just not doing them as effectively and efficiently as possible.

The good news: Once you're familiar with the steps of the money management program outlined in Part II, the actual amount of time you'll need to spend tracking your money will definitely *decrease.* Three and a half hours twice a month is our suggestion for beginners. Once you get the hang of tracking, you will determine how much time you need—and believe us, it will probably be less than what you now need. So don't be put off by the amount of time we suggest. It's just a starting point.

Besides, aren't you worth investing a few hours in if that's what it takes to make you fully conscious about your finances and moving toward getting rich?

We thought so!

STRATEGIES FOR FINANCIAL SUCCESS: THE RICH AND GOLDIE BANKS COMPANY

To help you get started, we've designed a form we call: Monthly Strategies for Financial Success. This checklist supports you in completing the tracking you'll need to do over the course of a month. (You'll probably need two sessions a month.)

As an example, on page 214 you'll find a sample of how our friends Rich and Goldie Banks use this checklist. Rich and Goldie have listed 12 activities that they want to complete during the month. As they finish each one, they place a check mark in the box on the far right. This way, at a glance, they know exactly what they have left to do.

On page 237 there's a blank checklist. This is yours to photocopy and use each month to monitor your strategies for financial success.

As we've said before, the guidelines we're suggesting are just that: suggestions. The exact content of your program is up to you. However, if you're not sure how best to begin, try starting with the program exactly as we've outlined. Then as you become more comfortable, you can customize the program as you go along.

Remember, what's at stake is your life's precious energy. Since you're expending it every minute anyway, why not make *every minute count* for you? You're worth it! You deserve it!

Most important, please remember to positively reward yourself for every success along the way. Every time you do your eight

MENTAL TIP ▐▼▼▼▼▼▼▼▼▼▼▼▼▼▼▼▼▼▼▼▼▼▼▼▼▼▼▼▼▌

 As you practice and become more efficient with Your Personal Money Management System, you'll find yourself spending less and less time tracking your money and more time mentally creating your Financial Freedom.

▐▼▼▼▼▼▼▼▼▼▼▼▼▼▼▼▼▼▼▼▼▼▼▼▼▼▼▼▼▌

minutes, thank and appreciate yourself. Every time you complete a tracking activity, tell yourself how proud and thankful you are. Why? More than almost anything, this bolsters your self-esteem and lays the foundation for a track record of financial success.

REMEMBER THE MOST IMPORTANT WORD: *NOW!*

Each time you put off something by promising to do it in the future, you're actually making a decision to *not* do it now.

And that seemingly benign procrastination can have malignant results.

For example, let's say it's time to balance your checkbook but you opt for going to the movies instead. Or it's time to figure your Monthly Expense Spreadsheet, but you put it off until next week because, well, you've just *got to* do your laundry tonight, and tomorrow there's a great golf tournament on TV, and the next night you're scheduled to play cards.

Know what you're doing?

You're directing your Private Access Learning System (PALS) that you do *not* really want the financial success you say you do. And guess what your PALS will give you in return? Just what they think you're asking for—financial failure.

On the other hand, if you choose to take action *now*, you're programming your PALS that you mean what you say. You're declaring that you *know* you're the President of a million-dollar company—and that you fully intend to *act* in such a way that your company achieves *maximum success.*

YOUR FINAL CHOICE

If, after reading this book, you're moved to begin the Financial Freedom program, there's only one choice available to you.

We think it's best summed up in this quote from the German writer Johann Wolfgang von Goethe.

Whatever you can do, or dream you
can, begin it.
Boldness has genius, power and magic
in it. Begin it now!

THE BANKS FAMILY'S MONTHLY STRATEGIES FOR FINANCIAL SUCCESS

DATE _____

1. Gratefully completing my Annual Income Summary Spreadsheet, listing all income received!	
2. Joyfully paying myself first!	
3. Gratefully paying my bills on time! Saving late charges!	
4. Easily balancing my bank statement!	
5. Enthusiastically completing my Monthly Expense Spreadsheet!	
6. Accurately completing my categories on the Annual Expense Summary Spreadsheet!	
7. Evaluating whether my expenditures are above or below my monthly projections by completing the "Keeping Score" section of my Annual Income Summary Spreadsheet.	
8. Planning any course corrections necessary for next month.	
9. Acknowledging and appreciating myself for implementing my Financial Freedom program.	
10. Having an uplifting Financial Freedom meeting with my family.	
11. Tracking the progress of my investments and entering asset income on my Annual Income Summary Spreadsheet!	
12. Tracking the reduction of my debts as I watch them go to zero!	

KEEPING SCORE

Your Wealth-
Building Forms

To maximize the user-friendliness of the material contained in this book, we suggest that you go to your local photocopying center and make enlarged copies of the forms and spreadsheets you'll need to implement Your Personal Money Management System. You'll find all the templates on the pages that follow, in the order in which they appear in the book. You may want to carefully make a master copy of each from the book and then make your enlargements from those.

In case you want to make them all at once, below is a complete list of all the forms as well as the sizes you'll want to enlarge to and also how many you'll need for a year's supply.

1. Current Assets. One copy (enlarge 129 percent to 8½ × 11 inches). Use only at the beginning of the program.

2. Current Debt Assessment. Two copies (enlarge 129 percent to 8½ × 11 inches). Use to track debt. Some **217**

people like to do this every month, and others, every few months. Use the first now, and save the second to make additional copies as needed.

3. Net Worth. Two copies (enlarge 129 percent to 8½ × 11 inches). Use at the beginning of the program and annually. Use the first now, and save the second to make additional copies annually.

4. Current Cash Flow. Two (enlarge 129 percent to 8½ × 11 inches). Use at the beginning of the program and annually. Use the first now, and save the second to make additional copies annually.

5. Annual Income Summary Spreadsheet. Two copies (enlarge 129 percent to 11 × 17 inches). The same form is used throughout the year, so use the first now, and save the second to make additional copies annually.

6. Worksheet for Monthly Expense Categories (with categories specified). One copy (enlarge 129 percent to 8½ × 11 inches). Use to assist you in establishing your monthly expense categories.

7. Worksheet for Monthly Expense Categories (blank). One copy (enlarge 129 percent to 8½ × 11 inches). An alternative to the category-specific version; you can write in whatever categories fit best for you.

8. Monthly Expense Spreadsheet. 15 to 20 copies (enlarge 129 percent to 11 × 17 inches). Use at least one spreadsheet every month, depending upon the number of checks you write and the number of categories you have.

9. Annual Expense Summary Spreadsheet. Three copies (enlarge 129 percent to 11 × 17 inches). The same form is used throughout the year, so use two now, and save the third to make additional copies annually.

10. Year-End Wrap-Up. Two copies (enlarge 129 percent to 8½ × 11 inches). Use once a year. Save the second to make additional copies annually.

11. Assets Tracking Form. Two copies (enlarge 129 percent to 8½ × 11 inches). Use once a year. Save the second to make additional copies annually.

12. Ideal Scene for Assets. Two (enlarge 129 percent to 8½ × 11 inches). Use once a year. Save the second to make additional copies annually.

13. Ideal Scene for Cash Flow. Two copies (enlarge 129 percent to 8½ × 11 inches). Use once a year. Save the second to make additional copies annually.

14. Daily Strategies for Creating Wealth. 20 copies (enlarge 129 percent to 8½ × 11 inches). Use one every week to clarify your eight-minute-a-day strategies.

15. Monthly Strategies for Success. Four (enlarge 129 percent to 8½ × 11 inches). Use one every month to identify your actions for the following month.

CURRENT ASSETS

_____

(date)

TOTAL ASSETS [_____]

CURRENT DEBT ASSESSMENT

_____

(date)

Owed to	Amount Owed	Annual Interest Rate	Minimum Monthly Payments	Payments Remaining
Totals				

NET WORTH

_____
(date)

TOTAL ASSETS [   ]

TOTAL DEBTS   [   ]

NET WORTH   [   ]

CURRENT CASH FLOW

ESTIMATED

ESTIMATED INCOME   ESTIMATED EXPENSES

(WEALTH-BUILDING ACCOUNT)

TOTAL INCOME	
TOTAL EXPENSES	
ANNUAL NET	
MONTHLY NET	

ANNUAL INCOME

YEAR		MONTHLY PRO-JECTIONS	JAN.	FEB.	MAR.	APR.	MAY
1							
2							
3							
4							
5							
6							
7							
8							
9							
10							
11							
12							
13							
14							
15							
16							
17							
18							
19							
20							
21							
22							
23							
24							
25							
26							
27							
28							
29							
30							

SUMMARY SPREADSHEET

JUNE	JULY	AUG.	SEPT.	OCT.	NOV.	DEC.	TOTALS	AVERAGE PER MONTH	
									1
									2
									3
									4
									5
									6
									7
									8
									9
									10
									11
									12
									13
									14
									15
									16
									17
									18
									19
									20
									21
									22
									23
									24
									25
									26
									27
									28
									29
									30

YOUR WORKSHEET FOR MONTHLY EXPENSE CATEGORIES

	1	2	3	4	5	6	7	8	9	10	11	12
MONTHLY FIXED EXPENSES												
Mortgage/Rent												
Real Estate Taxes												
Homeowner's Insurance												
Auto Insurance												
Health Insurance												
Life Insurance												
Auto Loan Payment												
Other Loan Payments												
MONTHLY VARIABLE EXPENSES												
Utilities												
Auto Repairs												
Telephone												
Education												
Groceries												
Clothing												
Personal Care												
Travel/Vacation												
Recreation												
Gifts												
Household Assistance												
Gasoline												
Health Care												
Donations												
Laundry/Cleaning												
Furnishings												

YOUR WORKSHEET FOR MONTHLY EXPENSE CATEGORIES

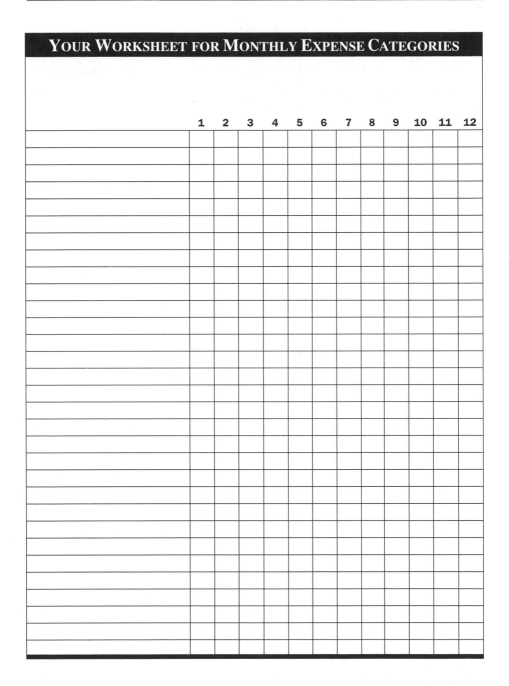

	1	2	3	4	5	6	7	8	9	10	11	12

MONTHLY EXPENSE

	DATE	CHECK #	TO	PAY YOURSELF FIRST (10% MINIMUM)				
1								
2								
3								
4								
5								
6								
7								
8								
9								
10								
11								
12								
13								
14								
15								
16								
17								
18								
19								
20								
21								
22								
23								
24								
25								
26								
27								
28								
29								
30								
			TOTALS					

Month _____ Year _____

SPREADSHEET										
								TOTAL	DEDUCT	
										1
										2
										3
										4
										5
										6
										7
										8
										9
										10
										11
										12
										13
										14
										15
										16
										17
										18
										19
										20
										21
										22
										23
										24
										25
										26
										27
										28
										29
										30

ANNUAL EXPENSE

YEAR _____ CATEGORY	MONTHLY PRO- JECTIONS	JAN.	FEB.	MAR.	APR.	MAY
1 Pay Yourself First						
2						
3						
4						
5						
6						
7						
8						
9						
10						
11						
12						
13						
14						
15						
16						
17						
18						
19						
20						
21						
22						
23						
24						
25						
26						
27						
28						
29						
30						
TOTALS						

SUMMARY SPREADSHEET

JUNE	JULY	AUG.	SEPT.	OCT.	NOV.	DEC.	TOTALS	AVERAGE PER MONTH	
									1
									2
									3
									4
									5
									6
									7
									8
									9
									10
									11
									12
									13
									14
									15
									16
									17
									18
									19
									20
									21
									22
									23
									24
									25
									26
									27
									28
									29
									30

YEAR-END WRAP-UP—_____

(annualized basis)

Income

$ _____	1. Salary
$ _____	2. Other business
$ _____	3. Interest or dividends used as income
$ _____	4. Other (list)
$ _____	5. Total income

Expenses

$ _____	6. Paid to myself and my family
$ _____	7. Other savings or retirement accounts
$ _____	8. Federal income taxes
$ _____	9. State income taxes
$ _____	10. Local taxes (if applicable)
$ _____	11. Social Security
$ _____	12. State disability insurance
$ _____	13. Remaining expenses
$ _____	14. Total expenses
$ _____	15. Total income
$ _____	16. Total expenses
$ _____	17. Net gain/loss for the year
$ _____	18. Amount added to Wealth-Building Account (sum of lines 6, 7 and possibly a portion of 17)
_____ %	19. Percentage added to Wealth-Building Account

ASSETS TRACKING FORM

_____
(date)

Asset	Current Value	Year-End Value

Totals

YOUR IDEAL SCENE FOR ASSETS

_____

(date)

TOTAL ASSETS	
TOTAL DEBTS	
NET WORTH	
ANTICIPATED GAIN	

YOUR IDEAL SCENE FOR CASH FLOW

_____
(date)

INCOME   EXPENSES

(WEALTH-BUILDING ACCOUNT)

TOTAL INCOME   [   ]
TOTAL EXPENSES   [   ]
ANNUAL NET   [   ]
MONTHLY NET   [   ]

DAILY STRATEGIES FOR CREATING WEALTH

ONE-MINUTE-A-DAY CHOICES	M	T	W	Th	F	Sa	Su
THREE-MINUTE-A-DAY CHOICES							

MONTHLY STRATEGIES FOR FINANCIAL SUCCESS

DATE _____

INDEX

Underscored page references indicate Management Tips and Mental Tips. **Boldface** references indicate illustrations, forms and spreadsheets.

FINANCIAL FREEDOM SEMINARS

Drs. Ron and Mary Hulnick are codirectors of the University of Santa Monica (USM), where Ron serves as president and Mary as academic vice-president.

USM offers master's degree programs in applied psychology and counseling psychology. The counseling psychology program fulfills the educational requirements in California for the marriage, family and child counselor license. Both programs are unique in that they have an emphasis in spiritual psychology and are held in weekend format. In this way, all USM programs meet the continuing educational needs of adult learners, who, in fact, fly in from all parts of the country and even relocate from abroad.

USM also offers *Financial Freedom in 8 Minutes a Day* weekend seminars designed to provide participants with hands-on experience in implementing the Financial Freedom program. These seminars are held in Santa Monica as well as throughout the country.

For more information about USM and its programs focusing on spiritual psychology or the *Financial Freedom in 8 Minutes a Day* seminar, please write or call: University of Santa Monica, 2107 Wilshire Boulevard, Santa Monica, CA 90403; (310) 829-7402.